40 lessons in

Of God's Grace.

Charity M. Jumbo

Published

by

Kratos Publisher

40 Lessons in 40 years of God's Grace

Copyright © 2022 by Charity M. Jumbo

Published by: Kratos Publisher

ISBN: 9798877544994

Foreword

Life's challenges, though arduous, hold lessons crafted by our Creator to mould us into vessels of honour, prepared for the Master's purpose. In these chapters, Charity takes you on a profound journey of self-discovery. From seeking validation and navigating complex relationships to encountering God's limitless mercies. Each lesson resonates with our pursuit of identity, interwoven with a deep yearning to draw closer to God.

May these lessons serve as an inspiration, guiding you toward introspection and understanding as you discover the divine treasures of healing divine.

Pastor Michael Ofori
Fountain Gate Chapel
Renown Pastures
Richmond, Virginia. USA

Foreword

Nothing is for nothing; everything is for something. What we think is a loss might be a gain, and what we think is a gain might be a loss.

A careful balance in life as we relate to God, with the wisdom and knowledge acquired will lead us to the place of success.

May our hearts be protected and may our mind be fruitful. Amen

God Bless You all.

Bishop Dr. Victor Osei

CONTENT

Contents

40 Lessons in 40 in Years | 7

Acknowledgement

To my Lord and Master Jesus, I am forever grateful for choosing me, enabling me, and ordering my steps through it all. The God who never disappoints; You stick till the end. You were there before I knew who you were. Thank you.

To my parents, Mr Eric Ekow Jumbo and Ms Adwoa Mensah, thank you for birthing me, covering me with your love and cheering me on as I climb. I'm grateful.

Mr Emmanuel and Rose Sally Owusu, you took me in as yours, and nurtured me till I understood boundaries. You covered me till I could fly on my own. Thank you for giving me the module on marriage and family. You created a safe space for me. Thank you.

To my father in the Lord, Bishop Dr Victor Osei, General Overseer of Family Chapel

International, Susanso, Kumasi Ghana, thank you for being my foundation in the Lord. You taught me well. I grew stronger spiritually because of you, and I couldn't ask for a better home. Thank you.

My Pastor, spiritual covering and mentor, Pastor Mario Ajavon of Todah City Church Coventry, UK. Me knowing and meeting you is divine. Words alone cannot describe how grateful I am to you for being there for me as I embarked on my healing journey. Thank you for creating the space for me to thrive and cheering me on as I learn from my mistakes to become God's ordained purpose. I appreciate you, my Man of God.

Godwin Emmanuel Atta Boafo, our paths crossing was not a mistake. The enemy failed in its quest; they meant it for evil, but God turned it around for good. Thank you for allowing the grace over your life to rub on me. You saw more than I saw in myself, so you called me Obaapa (a good woman).

PREFACE

Psalms 135:4 NLT

For the Lord has chosen Jacob for himself, Israel for his own special treasure.

I have realised that, regardless of our past, our life lessons should be carried forward into the future, which sets the next phase of our life. This can only occur if we choose to look at our experience from the trajectory of faith and not defeat. Some of these experiences might be painful, and some painless, but none are pointless. How we frame the stories we tell ourselves about yesterday sets the course of our tomorrow.

Considering these, I have concluded that none of these was an error; these occurrences model our perception of life, understanding that nothing just happens.

Ministry does not begin when we are ordained with a title. It begins the moment we give our life to Christ. The moment Jesus becomes our Lord and personal Saviour. Right from that moment, we become disciples of Jesus, a representation of him on earth.

Scripture clarifies that God begets us spiritually in His image, intending that we ultimately become the same kind of beings He and Jesus Christ are. The spirit-begotten Christian is a child of God, an actual member of the God family, but not yet in the ultimate sense. As Children, we must still go through development, processing this life, a period of building Godly character and becoming more like Him.

Adopted onto Sonship means there is an expectation to exhibit His intentions through the help of the Holy Spirit, calling us into His righteous purpose. If we continuously align ourselves to His ways, remain obedient to His instructions, and are willing to submit ourselves to Him, then ministry has begun.

The burdens He places on our hearts determine our direction of calling. If we continuously align ourselves to the ways of Jesus Christ, and accept to walk in obedience, believing He is the only way to our destination.

Matthew 4:19 NLT

Jesus called out to them, "Come, follow me, and I will show you how to fish for people!'

Romans 8:15 KJV

For ye have not received the spirit of bondage again to fear; but ye have received the Spirit of adoption, whereby we cry, Abba, Father.

This is the narrative of my life to reflect God's original purpose for me, and I am glad to share it with you.

INTRODUCTION

The notion that life begins at forty is accepted; some believe it is a myth, while others accept it as a Fact. Forty, midway to life expectancy, indicates that people of this age should have been fully accomplished in their career and family life. They should have developed the skill of making better decisions and judgements. This might be different for everyone as our journey in life is different, and our thought process varies.

Prophetically, forty is the number of trials/tests. It is either the beginning of a trying season or an overcoming season. Jesus fasted for forty days and was in the wilderness before the crucifixion. Israel was in the wilderness for forty years until the Lord delivered and led them to the promised land. This means the number of our days is very significant to our assignment. The numbers are counted according to God's calendar, not ours. That is why a younger person, in the natural sense, can begin ministry very early than an adult. God's purpose is not bound by age but by time/season. When that set time is due, no matter how old you are, you have begun according to God's timing.

Towards the end of 2019, while in worship at the domestic violence refuge centre, the Lord laid on my heart to write down my testimonies as a book. He gave me the title and specific instructions on how to write it. I asked, why me? He responded that it is not just about you but also the generations to come. I said, I am not qualified for this, and he replied, you have been qualified. I turn the unqualified into the qualified. This is for them to know of my goodness, not only to you but to all who will walk in my will, for them to trust me as they walk with me so that they will know that I am their God and there is none other. They will know I am the God who changes destinies, and if they continuously walk in obedience, they will eat the fruit of the land, and will

40 Lessons in 40 in Years | 15

understand that the definition of who they are is found in me, not in anything except me, God.

In obedience, I am sharing lessons I have learned in my last forty-years of walk with God. It has always been a challenging journey, full of ups and downs. It began with finding who I was, who I am in God, and why God chose me despite my weaknesses and disqualifications. I trust this autobiography will bless you as you journey in faith with me.

It's amazing to know how God's goodness can lead us to a disturbing and unfamiliar destination yet find His finger in it. No wonder He said he formed the blacksmith who created the weapon; therefore, no weapon formed against us will escape His knowing. His goodness upholds, teaches, and heals us until we accomplish His intent.

Psalm 23:6 NLT

'Surely your goodness and unfailing love will pursue me all the days of my life, and I will live in the house of the Lord forever.'

This is where I find myself now after I had been crushed and undergone discomfort, uncertainties, disappointments, and heartbreaks. I now understand that I have been chosen for his delight, and I have found who I am in Jesus Christ, His love, the unfolding essence of Him creating me, and the intentions of His heart long before placing me in my mother's womb.

So that I might perfect that which he has created me to be, He began working on my heart from the inside out, for out of it flows the issues of life. My desires were channelled towards Him. Chasing after God's heart is my daily ambition, and working out my salvation with fear and trembling is my chosen path. This is not because I have fully perfected all but because his grace is enough for those who diligently seek Him.

Up to this point in my life, I can confidently confess that the Lord is good, and his mercy endures forever.

Psalm 136:1 KJV

O give thanks unto the Lord; for he is good: for his mercy endureth forever.

Philippians 3:12 NLT

I don't mean to say that I have already achieved these things or that I have already reached perfection. But I press on to possess that perfection for which Christ Jesus first possessed me.

CHAPTER 1: LOOKING FOR SELF

Lesson 1: We Are God's Special Creation

I reflect on my family background, which includes four siblings: two stepsiblings and one with whom I share a biological parent. My heritage blends Nigerian and Ghanaian cultures, mirroring my father's mixed ancestry. His father hails from Nigeria's River State, while his mother originates from Cape Coast, a city in Ghana's Central Region.

Most individuals originating from River State tend to have a fair complexion, and as a result, several of my family members also share this fair skin tone. Coming of age in the 1980s and 1990s within a traditional African household, fair skin was highly valued. So much so that individuals who did not meet their desired fairness often resorted to external methods such as bleaching creams to lighten their complexion. I was the darkest in my nuclear family, which I was not happy about, so I felt less regarded. I could not vocalise this concern or apply any as I was too young to lighten my skin.

This inferiority complex worsened anytime I met with other family members who, in my view, were privileged to take after my grandfather's complexion. I never felt a sense of belonging; I felt excluded from the family.

My immediate younger sister is fair in complexion, which aggravated my insecurities. I secretly didn't like her for many senseless reasons. I was just jealous of her complexion.

Being naturally dark in complexion compared to the rest, I felt out of place. Silently, I didn't like myself. I felt very unfortunate. Family gatherings felt like punishment because I knew comments about our complexion differences would provokingly resurface.

I began losing my confidence, affecting my persona and how I carried myself. I spoke less and felt no one would like me in my dark complexion. I was trapped in my confusion, but no one could rescue me from the wrong perceptions I had about myself.

Lesson

We are God's creation, formed in His own image according to His will and purpose. Therefore, that intent must be manifested.

Right from the beginning, God, in His purpose, created us to suit the assignment chosen for us before we knew it or knew Him. This implies that our emergence in life is based on his plan and for his pleasure. Everything about His creation is intentional, including our physiques, temperament, the family we come from, the occurrences that surfaced as we grew up and everything that concern us. Our build-up and capabilities were all designed intentionally to prove God's diversity of creation.

Therefore, don't allow your looks, size, skin colour or race to determine your composure in life.

Ephesians 2:10 NLT

For we are God's masterpiece. He has created us anew in Christ Jesus, so we can do the good things he planned for us long ago.'

God's intention is for us to be like him, created in His image, for us to represent Him on earth and to dominate every area of His agenda. He expects us to express that capacity to fulfil the purpose we have been created as we exhibit our rulership on earth.

The enemy is an expert in using fear and insecurity to derail us from our purpose by ensuring our focus is tuned to something else, neglecting the pursuit of God. He renders us incapable; he rubs us off our success; he handicaps our growth in attaining and living a prosperous life.

That is why, as children of God, we need to be deliberate on the things we focus on, the things we give attention to, and the things that take our time and energy. The things we invest in will either make or unmake us, and they will mould and influence us positively or negatively.

The only place to find rest and fulfilment is in the Lord Jesus. This world has nothing to offer, but the greatest gifts and love are found in him, for Christ in you the hope of glory.

Just remember, you were a purpose before you became a person. The way you were created is exactly how He wants you to look, and He declared that it was good.

Gen 1: 31 BSB

And God looked upon all that He had made, and indeed, it was very good. And there was evening, and there was morning— the sixth day.

Psalm 139:14 BSB

I praise You, for I am fearfully and wonderfully made. Marvellous are Your works, and I know this very well.

Lesson 2: Seeking Attention and The Need to Be Loved.

There was a lot of rivalry between my sister and me. The thought of my sister being more fortunate than I was did not end there; it went on till I began feeling unloved by my parents. I always felt treated differently. There was the thought that she received more attention than I did.

I was an unhappy child. I did not realise the need to communicate my feelings to my parents because I expected them to know better. The thought that I was brought from somewhere into the family seemed substantiated by their neglect to resolve sibling rivalry.

Most parenting style in an African home is different from the Western countries. The authoritarian style of parenting is a usual type where children are expected to adhere to instructions from their parents without asking questions, and failure to obey will result in severe punishment. Therefore, the stern responses I got from my parents because of how I treated my sister were nothing unexpected. That is how the culture allows it, especially in Nigeria, where we lived at the time. Sibling rivalry was barely noticed, and the impact of non-parental affirmation is underestimated.

LESSON

Growing up in an African home, parents didn't see the need to address sibling rivalry. It wasn't a topic of importance. Siblings would have to figure out how-to live-in harmony with each other.

What I couldn't identify with myself was love and self-worth. It somehow occurred to me that, to feel and receive love, I would have to give it intentionally.

Love is selfless, and it is patient and not self-seeking. It's an active display and compels us to put others' needs above ours. Love honours others and celebrates truth no matter how difficult it is to hear. It gives off self even when it doesn't feel like it. Love doesn't allow feelings to dictate its choices. Love is hopeful, persevering, and trusting. Loving people keeps hatred and apathy far from them.

1 Peter 4:8 NLT

Most important of all, continue to show deep love for each other, for love covers a multitude of sins.

Mark 12:29-31 NLT

Jesus replied, "The most important commandment is this: 'Listen, O Israel! The Lord, our God, is the one and only Lord. And you must love the Lord your God with all your heart, all your soul, all your mind, and all your strength.' The second is equally important: 'Love your neighbour as yourself.' No other commandment is greater than these."

1 Corinthians 13: 4-7 NLT

Love is patient and kind. Love is not jealous or boastful or proud or rude. It does not demand its way. It is not irritable, and it keeps no record of being wronged. It does not rejoice about injustice but rejoices whenever the truth wins out. Love never gives up, never loses faith, is always hopeful, and endures through every circumstance.

This is a lesson I had to learn that,

My Love for God and neighbour is paramount, and as a child who wants to walk with God and please him.

I can't hate secretly and claim to love God. Irrespective of the wrong done to me, I am mandated to relate and exhibit love.

It is important to resolve matters of the heart, especially when it involves a relative. It weighs us down, so we are unable to live in freedom. The rage from pain alone can impede our access to God's blessing if we allow it to consume us.

As it occurred to Abel and Cain, Cain, out of jealousy, killed his brother Abel because God rejected his substance.

Genesis 4:6-8 NIV

Then the Lord said to Cain, "Why are you angry? Why is your face downcast? If you do what is right, will you not be accepted? But if you do not do what is right, sin is crouching at your door; it desires to have you, but you must rule over it." Now Cain said to his brother Abel, "Let's go out to the field." While they were in the field, Cain attacked his brother Abel and killed him.

Gaining knowledge of this fact, I resolved in my heart and declared that my name is Love. I am love, so I will share love in whichever way I can. This remained ever since, till it's become me, Charity.

Lesson 3: Searching for Validation

I became an athlete, running 100 meters for my school. I was able to win a couple of the races. This was good for me since I managed to gain recognition and popularity in the school. It created a haven within. They called me "*Jumbo Omo Ghana*", meaning Jumbo the Ghanaian child since they knew about my mixed culture. I loved the winning sound, which increased my zeal to run. It was the only thing that made me proud of myself; at least, my self-esteem was fed.

On one occasion, we were having an inter-house sporting competition. I took my position on the field, about to start the race, intending to win. Just a few yards to the finishing point, I was crossed from behind, falling facedown and breaking my left arm. I still don't understand how it happened, but there I was; I couldn't get up to complete the race, and I couldn't move my arm too. My passion for racing expired.

I had POP (Plaster of Paris) on for months. In my thoughts, my source of identification had been taken. I was angry and felt useless.

This caused me to dissociate myself from others because I couldn't retain the recognition, I had accumulated for myself. The thought that I wasn't good at anything caused my sense of identity to drift off.

Lesson

As daughters of God, we must remember that our ultimate identity is not defined by culture, people's opinions, titles, positions, success, or the humiliation from society due to differentiation, exclusion, or worldly definition. Who we are is found in the love of God.

His seal of approval was when He declared that His creation was good. We should not be defined by what we do, rather, by who we are in God and who we represent in what we do. We are fearfully made and a royal priesthood. We were created by a God whose speciality includes perfection. We must exhibit Gods perfection in any space He has called us to, been the light. Don't allow the worldly definition to cripple God's definition of you. Look at yourself from the lens of His eyes, knowing that we are loved by Him, irrespective, just as a potter loves his creation.

By surrendering to Christ and coming to believe in his birth, death, and resurrection power, we should understand that the same power that raised Jesus from the grave lives in us. Therefore, we have free access to His strength whenever we fall short. Also, realise that we have been found by grace and there is nothing that can change the love of God towards us; as scripture says, no heights or lows can snatch us from the love of God, and nothing can change God's love towards us unless we decide to denounce Him as our God and choose not to walk with Him, even so, His love for us is still available to us.

It is the enemy who makes us feel unworthy of his love. Never underestimate yourself and how far God can take you if you walk in his covenant and love.

Romans 8:31-39 KJV

'What shall we then say to these things? If God is for us, who can be against us? He that spared not his own Son, but delivered Him up for us all, how shall he not with him also freely give us all things? Who shall lay anything to the charge of God's elect? It is God that justifieth. Who is he that condemneth? It is Christ that died, yea rather, that is risen again, who is even at the right hand of God, who also maketh intercession for us. Who shall separate us from the love of Christ? Shall tribulation, or distress, or persecution, or famine, or nakedness, or peril, or sword? As it is written, for thy sake we are killed all day long; we are accounted as sheep for the

slaughter. Nay, in all these things, we are more than conquerors through him that loved us. For I am persuaded, that neither death, nor life, nor angels, nor principalities, nor powers, nor things present, nor things to come, nor height, nor depth, nor any other creature, shall be able to separate us from the love of God, which is in Christ Jesus our Lord.'

1 John 4:15-16 BSB

If anyone confesses that Jesus is the Son of God, God abides in him, and he in God. And we have come to know and believe the love that God has for us. God is love; whoever abides in love abides in God, and God in him. In this way, love has been perfected among us, so that we may have confidence on the day of judgment; for in this world we are just like Him.

Lesson 4: My Angry Self

Anger became an alternative to express the lack and inabilities within me. Not only was I disappointed that I could no longer run and enjoy the popularity I became accustomed to, but it was also related to the fact that I was no longer seen. The easiest way to express it was by shifting blame. I felt the whole world was against me, so I needed to fight back. I was warring against myself in my head.

This made me aggressive to the extent that any little misunderstanding with friends irritated me, leading to a fight.

Parents and their children often followed me home to report my misconduct after a bloody fight. Since my mother is a nurse, there was hope she would dress the sore apologetically. This happened most of the time, and it was becoming a norm for my mum. No one would dare mess with me at school; they stayed away as much as possible, and I became a total nightmare to my parents for the constant reports.

My learning drifted down over time. I failed most of my exams, and teachers cared less since I wouldn't listen to behavioural corrections. I thought fluency in English was just enough, as I could express myself better than the average student in my school. Most of my colleagues would not like to hang out with me, except those who were similar in character to mine; we became a gang.

In conclusion, I became the trouble child no one would like to get closer to. I would be called a bully in today's definition.

LESSON

Have you ever felt like you were drowning in a crowd, felt invisible, wondering if you mattered to anyone? Perhaps you are saying to yourself, "I am just a number. I don't add up to the equation. I just came across as someone who is part of the mass. Nobody sees or cares, and to think that God cares is unimaginable.

Don't be mistaken. These are lies from the pit of hell. The lies the devil uses make you doubt God's love for you. You are not your fears or inabilities; you are who God says you are, LOVED.

I want to remind you of this marvellous Bible Verse, which says he has called you by your name; I have given you an honourable name though you have not known me.

Isaiah 45: 4 AMP

'For the sake of Jacob My servant, And of Israel My chosen, I have also called you by your name; I have given you an honorable name Though you have not known Me.

In fact, not only do you matter to God, but he knows you by name and doesn't take his eyes off you.

He knows everything about you. He sees all your actions and deeds. He even knows the number of hairs on your head. He discerns your needs even before your discovery. He watches when you get up and when you lie down.

Psalm 33: 13-15 NLT

The Lord looks down from heaven and sees the whole human race. From his throne he observes all who live on the earth. He made their hearts, so he understands everything they do.'

Matthew 10:30 NLT

'And the very hairs on your head are all numbered.

Psalms 139:4 NLT

You know what I am going to say even before I say it, Lord.'

Matthew 6:8 NLT

'Don't be like them, for your father knows exactly what you need even before you ask him! '

Romans 8:38-39 NLT

'For I am persuaded, that neither death, nor life, nor angels, nor principalities, nor powers, nor things present, nor things to come, nor height, nor depth, nor any other creature, shall be able to separate us from the love of God, which is in Christ Jesus our Lord.'

You are not a nobody or just a number. God loves you the same way he knows you personally and intimately. He watches you carefully, and his loving eyes are focused on you from every direction. There is nothing that can ever separate you from His love. You are loved with intent and specially created for his delight; nothing can replace that. When you wake up, know that you are God's special child.

Lesson 5: Becoming a Thief and a Truant

Forming a gang meant there was always something to be taken care of. Every bad idea felt good. We were always striding from place to place, vandalising, doing everything satisfying.

We were four in number. One of us lived just opposite my house. She was my main friend, and she lived with her grandmother, who was partially blind. My friend felt forgotten and uncared for. She was an orphan who wanted to be as normal as any other child, but her situation made it impossible.

My friend had a great influence on me. I consented to most of her bad suggestions as I felt she was all I had and didn't want to lose her friendship, so I succumbed to everything to gain her acceptance. I didn't mind getting into trouble for her sake if it made her happy.

We began stealing at some point in our friendship to meet her needs, especially food. Stealing was her only option to meet her needs. I will steal from our kitchen as I thought my mum might not agree to me giving out our things. We even stole from others whenever we visited a friend's home. She knew I wanted to maintain our friendship at all costs; hence, she would threaten me with ending our friendship if I didn't comply with her truant suggestions.

Skipping school became the next fun thing to do. We would walk around town, doing nothing; it felt like freedom. We would be climbing and plucking fruits from people's yards. We stole anything left unattended to. This behaviour continued for weeks until some family friends saw us in town and notified my mum about it.

My Mum, being a Nurse, worked from morning till late afternoon, considering we lived at the nurse's quarters; making the community hospitals close to our house, so she couldn't monitor my truant activity.

I came home very dirty and exhausted most times, hungry and sweaty. I would cry and lie in total denial of her querying where I have been, as she sensed something was going on.

My Dad, a banker, had access to new currencies, so I usually received new naira notes for my lunch in school. My friend would take the money from me and controlled what we used the money for. Sometimes, we never buy food, but she will keep the money to herself. Knowing this, I sometimes steal extra money for her, so I get to keep mine. I had mixed feelings about doing it but complied for our friendship's sake.

One day, we planned to steal money from my mum, since my dad had just returned and he usually gave her new currencies for my schooling, which my friend wanted us to steal before she used it. We knew Mum's routine, so the plan was to return home once she left for work. We went through the back door of our house into her bedroom. My friend helped me put up chairs to reach the top of Mum's wardrobe, where her money was kept. I reached for the money and as I was pulling it out, I heard my mum's voice, screaming and asking what we were doing. I couldn't get down quickly as my friend hurried out of the house. There I was, caught in the act. I knew the magnitude of punishment awaiting me for my behaviour when my dad returned from His workstation.

As my daddy parked his car in front of our house, my heart started beating and my stomach rumbled in fear. I couldn't run to meet him as usual; I was terrified. My sister went to meet him and then, she began narrating the whole incident. Oh, how I wanted to exclaim, shut up!

Mom added the details to the report and tears streamed down my cheeks. Unknown to me, my school had given Mum a report of my truancy. This added more fuel to the fire. It felt like a doom's day to me.

Daddy called me, he asked a simple question if it was true, but all I could say was "I am sorry, crying". Daddy took out his belt and I had a beating of my life. He concluded by saying I would be going with him to Okene, his workstation, which is in the Kogi State of Nigeria. I was not only going to be living with him, but obviously I would be changing my school as well.

It felt like my whole world was crushed that day, as my parents wouldn't allow me to go out, and I didn't get to say goodbye to my friends. It was the saddest weekend ever.

LESSON

John 10:10 NLT

The thief's purpose is to steal and kill and destroy. My purpose is to give them a rich and satisfying life.

The enemy aims at destroying the purpose God has destined for us. He wants to get us to the point where we will have no confidence in who God has created us to be. He aims to corrupt our character in conformation to His objective.

There is nothing good in the enemy's camp. His specialty is to distort God's goodies instilled in us.

He is full of lies and camouflage. He tried to turn me into something I was not, using lies of attachment to bind me to an ungodly relationship. His main aim was to cripple me into becoming a thief, rendering me unqualified of being a child of God so that the Lord's purpose for my life would be aborted. But little did he know that it was pushing me towards my destiny. **The valley prepares you for the mountain top. It is just the lower part of** the land between hills or mountains, which means getting to the top of the mountain is not far-fetched. The pain you are going through is propelling you into becoming the person God has called you to be and not destroying or punishing you in any way.

God did not allow the enemy's plan to manifest in my life. He is aware of the end right from the beginning. Only his plans for our life will stand and none other. The enemy wanted to use my God-given strength, which is a kind heart, a virtue necessary for the kingdom, as a weapon of destruction, but the God who knows our heart and who judges man did not allow that plan to surface. To him be all the praise.

Romans 6:16 NIV

Don't you know that when you offer yourselves to someone as obedient slaves, you are slaves of the one you obey—whether you are slaves to sin, which leads to death, or to obedience, which leads to righteousness?

The enemy wants us to yield, for him to enslave us successfully, but thanks be to God Almighty who died on the cross in exchange for my liberation.

John 8:34 NLT

Jesus replied, "I tell you the truth, everyone who sins is a slave of sin.

Jeremiah 1:5 NLT

"I knew you before I formed you in your mother's womb. Before you were born, I set you apart and appointed you as my prophet to the nations."

Romans 6: 12-14

Do not let sin control the way you live; do not give in to sinful desires. Do not let any part of your body become an instrument of evil to serve sin. Instead, give yourselves completely to God, for you were dead, but now you have new life. So, use your whole body as an instrument to do what is right for the glory of God. Sin is no longer your master, for you no longer live under the requirements of the Law. Instead, you live under the freedom of God's grace.

Lesson 6: Living with Dad

As we approached the city of Okene, I realised its beauty and modernity were different from where we lived in Inisa. The town had beautiful streets, lights, houses and cars of different shapes and sizes, some of which I had never seen.

Inisa is found in Osun State of Nigeria, a little town where most houses were built with clay, bricks, and others with cement in the mid-80s. Most people were farmers and traders. The town only had a clinic, and my mum was the head medical practitioner then. She loved her career and was always ready to help. Everyone knew us.

It felt like things would be different here in Okene as I didn't know anyone. This new environment was terrifying to me. Nothing seemed familiar except Daddy.

That evening, we went out to eat with some of Daddy's friends. I was usually quiet and very observant as many things were unusual to me, I didn't understand a thing and was not conversant with their food, attitudes, and dialect.

As time passed, I became confident as a lot became comprehensible, and I began engaging in conversations. Daddy would take me everywhere...to the mechanics, shops, visiting friends, etc. He would ask me questions from time to time that would generate conversation. Daddy became my new friend as we began bonding. He literally replaced my old friends.

There were unfamiliar things in my new environment which I was eager to accommodate. I am beginning to prefer the new me to my previous lifestyle. The thought of my friend never resurfaced.

Lesson

We are God's handiwork. He channels our life to suit the destination and his purpose for us. He determines when it's finished and when a new page begins. He's the author and finisher of our faith. Hebrew 12:2

From this, we can deduce that Christ is the originator of our faith, He begins it, as well as captains our faith into maturity. This indicates that Jesus, through the Holy Spirit, embodies our faith, our understanding, and thoughts. He steers it as a captain steers a ship and presides over it till it thrives.

Just by changing my environment, my desires changed, my friends and perspectives altered, including the things that were of importance to me. I no longer felt the need to prove anything. Rather, I felt too little in my new environment and was eager to be part of it.

I was interested in anything that would broaden my understanding of how things worked around here. Thank God for my father, who was constantly teaching and correcting, which changed my mentality. I felt empowered rather than belittled.

God uses people, situations, and our environment to influence the truth and lies we endorse in our spirit. Be sensitive to these things; they determine how far you will get in your life journey. Whoever you allow into your space can either propel you or be a distraction. Be vigilant.

Ephesians 2:10 KJV

For we are his workmanship, created in Christ Jesus unto his good works, which God had before ordained that we should walk in them.

Genesis 2:8 NLT

Then the Lord God planted a garden in Eden in the east, and there he placed the man he had made.

Just as God perfected what he created, Eden was the perfect environment for God's first intention for mankind i.e. to be fruitful, multiply and to become what he purposed in his heart for Man's advancement.

Eden, for you may be a situation, an unfavourable condition that will transform you into God's intention. He rectifies, and restructures the posture of our heart, our cultural perspective and ideology to suit our journey.

Eden seasons differ from person to person depending on what needs constructing and pruning. It is a place of seclusion, where character is developed and built. In Eden, we experience the visitation and presence of God. We get to commune with him and understand His will.

Don't underestimate your current circumstance, it's necessary for your destination. Learn from it, it becomes a key; for nothing goes waste in God.

John 6:12 NLT

After everyone was full, Jesus told his disciples, "Now gather the leftovers, so that nothing is wasted."

Lesson 7: Connection with Daddy

Going to live with Dad was the best decision he took. It changed a lot of things in me including my relationship with him. He became aware of his willingness to parent compared to knowing of his fatherhood. He taught me a lot of soft skills, he listened to me read and corrected my pronunciations and spellings. He paid attention to everything I did. Our relationship as father-daughter grew stronger. He called me by whistling through his mouth, which was my favourite of Him.

I saw him differently from how I knew him to be. He graduated from being just a disciplinarian to a friend. I felt secure, protected, loved, and cared for. I did not need to prove anything because he consistently affirmed me. Everything about me was perfect to him to the extent that he mentioned it to his friends, and they would laugh over it. I tried picking up the language, and they would laugh over my pronunciation. It felt like having a father for the first time. Nothing can separate us from the love of our Parents. I was my daddy's "little girl."

Lesson

John 10: 25-30 NLT

Jesus replied, "I have already told you, and you don't believe me. The proof is the work I do in my father's name. But you don't believe me because you are not my sheep. My sheep listen to my voice; I know them, and they follow me. I give them eternal life, and they will never perish. No one can snatch them away from me, for my father has given them to me, and he is more powerful than anyone else. No one can snatch them from the father's hand. The Father and I are one."

When in God's radial, he keeps you secured under his wings. He ensures your needs are met, and he carries you on his shoulder, ensuring your foot does not hit any stone.

If we have God Lording over our life, and we choose to strengthen our relationship continuously, victory over the enemy is inevitable.

Only when you remain under his shelter, and you make the Lord your God that your shelter remains.

Psalms 91:9-12 NLT

If you make the Lord your refuge, if you make the Most High your shelter, no evil will conquer you; no plague will come near your home. For he will order his angels to protect you wherever you go. They will hold you up with their hands, so you won't even hurt your foot on a stone.

Lesson 8: Daddy and I

Daddy takes me to his office after school, where I spend my afternoons. I do my homework, have lunch, and relate with other colleagues of his, including their children.

They send me on errands, moving from one department to the other, whether collecting a file or delivering office stationery. This was normal in the mid-eighties as most of their banking practices were manually carried out. There were no computers then, internal communication was by word of mouth. They used ledger books and papers for most of their banking work, considering this being Africa, where development was still underway.

I got to make friends with other kids who were brought to the office from school. I was exposed to the office environment and fell in love with it. The seed of becoming a banker began right from there. I enjoyed the office work even though I did not

58

understand what they did. All I knew was that people brought money into the bank, and we also gave money out to people.

My daddy was an accountant then, so he sometimes stayed till late, making sure that they balanced, i.e., money collected matched with the accompanying paperwork, meaning I would stay till it was completed.

As much as this was fun, it affected my sleeping pattern as I would have to wake up early in the morning for school and go to bed late. I dozed off in class mostly and could not concentrate on my studies.

I had challenges in learning due to my change from a public school to an international school. The educational standard of the private school was higher than my previous public school. I was not conversant with many things, including some of the topics previously taught in the class. This made me lag in class and did not encourage learning.

On one occasion, we had a class test, and I had all the answers wrong, so the teacher wrote my zero mark over ten on the sheet. He then drew a pair of ears and eyes on the zero mark with a red pen, indicating those were mine in my workbook. Daddy got very irritated and reported it to the head teacher. They told Dad of my inability to catch up with the rest and their concerns that I was always sleeping in class and unable to understand things at the level I was.

On hearing this, Daddy had to decide how to make me get enough rest and how to help with my studies as well. His friend suggested I go with his children to their house when their mother picked them up from the office so I could have some rest. He also suggested that I join their kids in the extra lessons received after school with a private teacher, so Dad agreed I join them, and then he would pick me up after work.

This became a new routine, which I wouldn't say I liked because I always felt out of place there. The kids did not like the idea of joining them and were mean to me, and so was their mother. But in the African community at the time, the father made most of the decisions for the family, which they had to comply with. Their mother could not turn down the idea, but she could not voice it out either.

I complained several times to Daddy, but he had no option but for me to hang in there. He told me he would not know where to take me if I did not manage with them. The painful part was I sometimes spent the weekend there as Daddy would have to go to work meetings. I guess he also needed some time to be alone.

As much as the classes helped, I could not perform to capacity because I felt rejected by the kids. Most children in my class did not like me for one reason or the other. I could not fit in. My teacher did not like me much because Daddy reported him to the head teacher, so I had no hiding place in school.

As time progressed, my results in school improved. I could mingle better with the kids in my class. Daddy reduced my time for extra classes to thrice a week compared to every day of the week. We all adjusted somehow to this schedule.

Lesson

In John 3:16, The Bible states that for God so loved the world that he gave his only begotten son. The love of God for his children is such that he consistently gives us things that pertain to life, things that express his love towards us. He gives us everything that will bring us to a place of sustenance, where our hunger is fed and where we can identify with his glory. Everything about the Christian walk is giving and receiving. You can't express your love to someone and are unwilling to give to them in the measure you believe will satisfy their need.

John 3:16 NLT

"For this is how God loved the world: He gave his one and only Son, so that everyone who believes in him will not perish but have eternal life.

I could identify my daddy's expression of love in my story, where he had a decision to make by incorporating his work and his desire for my success. It might not be the perfect choice, but that is his limitation as a human, yet to the best of his knowledge and capability, he expressed love for his child.

Our God Jesus Christ expressed love by giving us His only precious son that if we continue to believe in Him, and trust in his commands, we will have eternal life and not perish. Everything needed for eternal life is found in his obedience and in giving ourselves to him by submitting to his authority. The Bible says he loved us even before we knew him 1 John 4:19.

He expressed his love for us even before we became acquainted with him before we became conscious of who we are in Christ. He was already in love with us, and his expression of love towards us got us to the place of realising we wouldn't have qualified to be in oneness with him if not for His love towards us.

1 John 4:19 NLT

We love each other because he loved us first.

This shows us that, with every expression of love we show our fellow human beings, whether related or not, we are emulating the love Christ Jesus had instilled in us. The more you spend time with God by walking in his precepts, the more you can extend the hand of love without waiting for a reward. Christ is love, and all who dwell in Christ dwell in love.

1 John 4:16-17

We know how much God loves us, and we have put our trust in his love. God is love, and all who live in love live in God, and God lives in them. And as we live in God, our love grows more perfect. So, we will not be afraid on the day of judgment, but we can face him with confidence because we live like Jesus here in this world.

In conclusion, **I want to assure you that his love will secure and protect you. All he needs from us is for us to trust in this love and be willing to receive it, trusting him and be in obedience to his commandments.** John 14:15 places the ball in our court. If we love him, we will obey his commandments. You cannot be in union with something you have no love for.

John 14:15 NLT

"If you love me, obey my commandments.

As you prove in obeying his commandments and have chosen to walk in his precepts, he sends the Holy Spirit to teach us which way to go, an advocate who will never leave us and leads us to all truth. V.21 of John 14 states that because we have accepted and obeyed his commandments, we have proven to love him back and he then reveals himself to us. Destiny is unfolded as you continue to commune with God in love, and you unravel into destiny.

John 14:21 NLT

Those who accept my commandments and obey them are the ones who love me. And because they love me, my father will love them. And I will love them and reveal myself to each of them."

Lesson 9: Understanding My Environment

As time went on, I became aware of my circumstances. I navigated my day-to-day activities without arguments, though sometimes my reactions weren't the best. Dad explained the condition we were in and what it meant for us to adjust to the new arrangement, clarifying that it would bring about a comfortable life.

In agreement with that, it was then necessary for me to put up my best behaviour anytime I went to our friends. I would isolate myself as much as I could to avoid trouble. I stopped complaining to Dad to put him at peace. I felt out of place for succumbing to this decision of not wanting to infuriate Dad's friend. It was pressurising not to voice out.

After constant pretence, I developed the skill of controlling my temper. I became extremely calm.

I agreed to everything even when I didn't want to. I discomforted myself to make others happy to avoid being the troublesome one as I was made to believe.

LESSON

God made us for relationships and made relationships for us. He created us to connect with him as we connect with others. Despite the fractures that can occur from differences of perspective, friendship is truly one of God's greatest gifts to us.

When we're deeply hurt, we may define our journey by the pain suffered, altering our course, scaling back our dreams, or abandoning them altogether. We may believe the enemy's definition of who we are consciously or subconsciously.

An emotional trauma cuts deeply into our souls painfully because it is unexpected. It hits when our defences are down, and our trust levels are low. It is critical to understand that when people choose to leave us, God never leaves. He knows how it feels to be kicked in the gut, to have the wind knocked out of us, and he cares. He promises to be there for us and even when people try to be faithful. Remember, the faithfulness of God is ever sure.

Psalm 34:18 MSG

If your heart is broken, you'll find God right there; if you're kicked in the gut, he'll help you catch your breath.

Hebrew 13:5 AMP

Let your character [your moral essence, your inner nature] be free from the love of money [shun greed—be financially ethical], being content with what you have; for He has said, "I will never [under any circumstances] desert you [nor give you up nor leave you without support, nor will I in any degree leave you helpless], nor will I forsake or let you down or relax My hold on you [assuredly not].

Embracing all the unexpected adventures we come across, we are created to do life with people. It is necessary to build and nurture relationships not withstanding their propensity of hurting us.

We need not forget that some people are sent purposely to help us, we just need to guard our hearts and be vulnerable enough to accommodate their presence and the transformation that comes with change.

Proverbs 4:23 NLT

Guard your heart above all else, for it determines the course of your life.

Lesson 10: A New Page is Turned

Our day began as usual; Dad picked me up from school and went to his workplace. Everything was going well until the day seem unending. I slept and woke up, yet he was still in a meeting. I was later told that he had been promoted to the position of a bank manager. This promotion came with a transfer to Ogbomosho, in the Oyo State of Nigeria.

A few months before this, Mum had been transferred to Oshogbo in the Osun State of Nigeria, which meant they would change where I lived and schooled, either with Dad in Ogbomosho or with Mum in Oshogbo.

The time came for us to leave Okene. A send-off party was organised for Daddy by his colleagues, and we were able to bid everyone goodbye. We went to Oshogbo where Mum is now living. It was a moment of family reunion for us, as we hadn't seen ourselves in a long while.

Oshogbo is a beautiful city with a larger population than the little town Mum was living in Inisha. There were modern buildings and beautiful roads, just like Okene. Compared to my previous environment, most things were familiar now. The language was not a problem as I can speak the Yoruba language. I was quite happy with where we lived, which matched my current exposure.

It was confirmed I will be staying with Mum while Daddy would be coming from his station every weekend.

Mummy resumed work. I had been enrolled in a new school, made friends, and adjusted to my new environment perfectly.

Lesson

Location is one of the means God uses in reaching out to us.

He leads us on a path known to him alone, where he can reach us where his provision is available to meet our sustenance.

For this reason, it is paramount for a child of God to be obedient to God's direction because until He finds you in His expected place, you won't find His glory, nor will his presence be reachable to you. As omniscient as our God is, He still moves according to principles and obedience and chooses where to meet us.

Adam and Eve were placed in a location (Garden of Eden) to tend and watch over the land (Gen 2:15) so that they were reachable and that He could commune with them. This does not imply inability to reach them, but by his principle, His purpose for their lives and how He chooses to relate with them. Our garden of Eden differs; it depends on how he communes with us as children. The Bible says in Genesis 3:8, that God would visit them in the cool of the day, until they fell.

Genesis 2:8 NLT

Then the Lord God planted a garden in Eden in the east, and there he placed the man he had made.

Genesis 2:15 NLT

The Lord God placed the man in the Garden of Eden to tend and watch over it.

Jeremiah 18:1-3 NLT

The Lord gave another message to Jeremiah. He said, "Go down to the potter's shop, and I will speak to you there." So, I did as he told me and found the potter working at his wheel. God spoke to Jeremiah to teach his naivety. This information required his intellect and his ability to comprehend what had been taught, which necessitated a specific location. **God can be anywhere but doesn't manifest everywhere. When you find that place, transformation is bound to take place.** Therefore, you can't afford to be anywhere as a child of God. Your location is as valuable as the lessons you will be taught, which is crucial to your assignment. It is also critical to ask and seek God's direction before making any move as a child of God. **Embrace your change in location when you finally discern your God-given direction.**

CHAPTER 2: FINDING SELF

Lesson 11: Salvation

Few months passed; Mum was promoted to one of the clinical heads of the local government. This required her to work away, including weekends, visiting clinics under her jurisdiction. There came the challenge of caring for myself and my junior sister while away. A house help was the next option.

One afternoon, mummy came home with this beautiful lady called Lola. I liked her the moment I saw her; she was calm and very friendly. She wasn't too old, probably in her late 20s or early 30s, I guess. She had a welcoming persona which was difficult to deny. I was happy to have her living with us.

Her love for the Lord was something that stood her out. She was always praying and reading her Bible. She would read the Bible to me and teach me the Bible. I would stare at her when she prayed even though I didn't understand what she was doing. It somehow felt good to behold, and I wanted to partake in it. She would pray for me and ask me to repeat some prayers. This practice was an eye-opener. I began to understand that there is a deity called God whom we should pray to.

As a family, we barely went to church, even when we did, it was for ceremonies such as weddings and naming ceremonies. Conclusively, Lola led me to Christ. She taught me much about God by sharing her Bible studies with me, and would correct me when I misbehaved, especially if it was unchristian. She taught me how to pray when she prays. Her Love for God was undeniable, and I emulated it as I got closer to knowing God.

Lesson

Don't underestimate the people God brings into your life. Their purpose is to propel you into attaining God's plan for you, for the Lord is our

shepherd who leads us in the path of our righteousness.

This includes sending people our way who are mandated to usher us towards his purpose by revealing the mysteries in God and His word.

What then is Salvation? It is the price paid by Christ in exchange for our freedom and redemption of our life. For us to be set free, a price had to be paid. But to whom? Jesus didn't pay it to the devil. He paid the price that God required to satisfy His holy justice.

According to Ezekiel 18:20, "The person who sins will die." The cost of our redemption was the blood of the perfect Son of God, and He made this sacrifice in our place. Because the Father accepted Christ's payment, we've been set free from bondage to sin and have received the power of the Holy Spirit, who enables us to live in the freedom of obedience to the Father.

Ezekiel 18:20-22 NLT

The person who sins is the one who will die. The child will not be punished for the parent's sins, and the parent will not be punished for the child's sins. Righteous people will be rewarded for their own righteous behaviour, and wicked people will be punished for their own wickedness. But if wicked people turn away from all their sins and begin to obey my decrees and do what is just and right, they will surely live and not die. All their past sins will be forgotten, and they will live because of the righteous things they have done.

No one can have a relationship with the heavenly Father if not for the blood of Jesus that speaks forgiveness and redemption. God's holiness cannot accommodate our sinfulness which disrupts our chance of connection with Him. However, for His love, He initiated a reconciliation course by allowing His son Jesus Christ to be exchanged for the fallen humanity, becoming sin in our place. **By the reason**

of the blood of Jesus, we can get close to the Father.

Jesus Christ was hanged on the cross by becoming a curse, for cursed is the one hanged on a tree (Gal 3: 13) redeeming us from the curse of sin. Maybe you think you're a pretty good person and don't feel enslaved to sin. But no matter how moral a person may seem; every human has a sinful nature. Rom. 3:23.

Romans 3:23 NLT

For everyone has sinned; we all fall short of God's glorious standard.

When it comes to forgiveness of our sins, we have the idea that the Lord will forgive us only because we asked Him. However, the basis for His pardon is Christ's payment for our debt with His blood which is the atonement for our sinfulness. The Lord does not forgive wrong only because we ask but because He had already forgiven us and have resolved to allow us to partake in His glory and the promise of his spirit if we ask in faith. Even when we were still sinners the Lord came to die. **His Holiness does not allow Him to overlook sin, and His justice will not let Him reject the punishment required for trespasses.**

With the substitutionary death of the perfect Son of God, does the Father have a legitimate basis by which He can forgive whoever comes to Him in faith and repentance Eph. 1:7. There is nothing we can do to earn His forgiveness. Our pardon is granted because Christ's blood is applied to our lives. The blood that speaks better words than that of Abel. The blood that atones and speaks redemption on our behalf and has given us the right to call Him Abba Father. Praise be to God.

Ephesians 1:7 NLT

He is so rich in kindness and grace that he purchased our freedom with the blood of his Son and forgave our sins.

Hebrews 12:24 NIV

To Jesus the mediator of a new covenant, and to the sprinkled blood that speaks a better word than the blood of Abel.

Romans 8:15 NIV

The Spirit you received does not make you slaves, so that you live in fear again; rather, the Spirit you received brought about your adoption to sonship. And by him we cry, "Abba, Father."

Lesson 12: I Found a Friend-Sister

Lola became my friend. I followed her everywhere, even when she was sent on errands. We were very close; I could share my thoughts easily and she would enlighten me as an adult would guide their younger siblings. Lola was just an embodiment of a pacesetter for me.

Lola showed me the foundation of what is expected of a child of God. She encouraged me as I journeyed in God and influenced my responses to situations in a Godly manner. I became aware that the Spirit of God dwells in our hearts, and we carry him everywhere.

The knowing that, there is a special treasure hidden in us was beyond imaginable. When I understood that He hates sin, I became conscious of my character, asking for forgiveness the moment I fall into sin.

Lesson:

Lola's friendship was divine. I believe she was sent my way for a purpose, for me to know Him. For me to find a friend in him through a friend. I never thought that kind of closeness could erase the damage caused by previous friends. The light Lola emanated, reflected on every darkness hidden within me. Now I'm a partaker of the light that lit the world.

Proverbs 18:24 AMP

The man of too many friends [chosen indiscriminately] will be broken in pieces and come to ruin, but there is a [true, loving] friend who [is reliable and] sticks closer than a brother.

It is not about how many friends you have access to, it's about the impact they make in your life. How can they channel you into the will and the purpose of God for your life? Are they influencing you positively or negatively? These questions need to be asked before getting acquainted with anyone. We must be aware of their mandate in our environment since we embody our influences, just like the computer terminology, "garbage in, garbage out". Therefore, as children of God, we should be aware of our environment as it can manipulate us.

Eve's deception began from the moment she engaged in a conversation with the serpent, even before getting to eating of the forbidden fruit. The serpent is referred to as crafty and skilled in deceit, more than any living creature of the field. Hence, he succeeded in beguiling Eve which resulted in them sinning against God.

Genesis 3:1-6 AMP

Now the serpent was more crafty (subtle, skilled in deceit) than any living creature of the field which the Lord God had made. And the serpent (Satan) said to the woman, "Can it really be that God has said, 'You shall not eat from any tree of the garden'?" And the woman said to the serpent, "We may eat fruit from the trees of the garden, except the fruit from the tree which is in the middle of the garden. God said, 'You shall not eat from it nor touch it, otherwise you will die.'" But the serpent said to the woman, "You certainly will not die! For God knows that on the day you eat from it your eyes will be opened [that is, you will have greater awareness], and you will be like God, knowing [the difference between] good and evil." And when the woman saw that the tree was good for food, and that it was delightful to look at, and a tree to be desired in order to make one wise and insightful, she took some of its fruit and ate it; and she also gave some to her husband with her, and he ate.

We realise that a simple conversation with the wrong person can mislead us on our journey. If we consistently allow God to lead us, yielding to the Holy Spirit, and grounded in the word of God, He will bring us to the right environment with the right people who are mandated for the path He

ascribed to us, for the Lord orders the steps of the righteous.

Psalm 37:23 GNT

The Lord guides us in the way we should go and protects those who please him.

Remember, if the world became sinful by one person, it also requires only one person to bring it back to life. That was why God had to send his only begotten son to redeem us from sin, to break the yoke of sin off us. This means, that just having the wrong people can compromise your character, which delays God's manifestations through you. Even though your sins will be forgiven when you repent, be vigilant, intentional with decisions and your choices, for they make you.

Lesson 13: Holy Spirit Encounter

It was an all-night service in Lola's Church, Christ Apostolic Church (CAC), Nigeria. I was allowed to go with her that day as I'm usually not allowed for all night's church services. Service went on till it was time for prayer. Everyone was seriously praying, and then Lola suddenly went under the spirit. She was speaking in a different language. Suddenly, the room was silent, and we listened to her speak. She interpreted as she spoke. I was in awe as I had never seen such a display. There was a heavy presence in the room. I felt something special had occurred at that moment.

I had another opportunity to be in a Sunday service with Lola. This time, I asked to go to the children's service. Service progressed from Bible studies to question time. I could not confidently respond to the questions asked but the new information from the Bible created a hunger for more. I constantly looked forward to hearing the word of God.

I was led to Christ that morning. They prayed for me and requested the baptism of the Holy Spirit to fill me up. I felt a heavy weight fall on me, which left me lying on the floor for a while. It was an unexplainable experience which brought excitement and unquenchable joy within me. I believed in what had occurred, and I knew that my totality had been changed.

Lesson

John 14:26 AMP

But the Helper (Comforter, Advocate, Intercessor—Counsellor, Strengthened, Standby), the Holy Spirit, whom the Father will send in My name [in My place, to represent Me and act on My behalf], He will teach you all things. And He will help you remember everything that I have told you.

He promised to be with us not physically as the disciples experienced but to be present in us, in our hearts, in the form of a Holy Spirit. He will speak to us, direct us, teach us and be as Jesus would have been if he were physically present. He is alive in us, dwelling daily till eternity. It only takes those who believe, receive, and obey his commandments who will experience the Holy Spirit.

John 14:16-17 AMP

And I will ask the Father, and He will give you another Helper (Comforter, Advocate, Intercessor— Counsellor, Strengthener, Standby), to be with you forever— the Spirit of Truth, whom the world cannot receive [and take to its heart] because it does not see Him or know Him. Still, you know Him because He (the Holy Spirit) remains with you continually and will be in you.

The Holy Spirit is likened to a network on a phone (sim card). It determines which signal to pick up depending on which network the owner is subscribed to. Without a sim card or a network, the phone is useless no matter how modern the phone is. This network allows the owner to make good use of the phone, which allows him access to the functionalities of the phone.

In the same way, Christians need the Holy Spirit to function. We can download data/information from the heavenly father, and He (Holy Spirit) communicates what is being instructed by our Father in heaven. We are privileged to speak the heavenly language, which the Spirit understands and can decode to our Father. A Child of God is incomplete without the Holy Spirit. That is what separates us from the ungodly.

The Holy Spirit does not only connect us with our heavenly father, He also allows us to produce good fruits that are evidence of our

connection with God. These are Love, Joy, Peace, Kindness, Faithfulness, Patience, Gentleness, Goodness, and Self-control.

Galatians 5:22-23 AMP

But the fruit of the Spirit [the result of His presence within us] is love [unselfish concern for others], joy, [inner] peace, patience [not the ability to wait, but how we act while waiting], kindness, goodness, faithfulness, gentleness, self-control. Against such things there is no law.

Lesson 14: Manifesting the Holy Spirit

Guess who is in Love. I have fallen in love with the God who loved and knew me before forming me in my mother's womb. He knew me long before I became acquainted with him. I am now redeemed, restored and a new creation in Christ Jesus. Praise the Lord.

I was conscious that I had the Holy Spirit dwelling in me whom I speak to, and He responds to me. I could not complete a task without asking the still voice within. He became the perfect friend that sticks closer than a brother. Prov.18:24.

As naive as I was in the things of God, my thoughts and choices were intentional. I wanted to be on the right, as much as possible, not to wrong the spirit. Lola was there to guide me through this stage. She was always reading the bible to me, praying with me, and guiding me as I took my baby steps toward God. She mentored me in the best way she could for me to understand and emulate.

Lola taught me to always listen to the still little voice within me. I should speak to him, and he would guide me through every step of life. The understanding that there was a spirit in Man that helps and guides was a breakthrough for me. It felt like I had a superpower that helped with everything.

I wanted to see if the Holy Spirit exists and if He helps. One day, I got into trouble which I knew would get me punished, so I looked for a way of preventing it from happening. I asked by praying that I get sick, to escape the punishment, and within a few minutes, I was down with a fever for about three days. And yes, I skipped the punishment. This was just one of the ways I confirmed that the Holy Spirit is real, and that He really helps. As creepy as this may sound, I know God allowed it to help me understand that He's capable of doing all things. He met me at my level of understanding. He just wanted me to trust Him.

Lesson

Ezekiel 36:27 NLT

And I will put my Spirit in you so that you will follow my decrees and be careful to obey my regulations.

The spirit that comes to dwell in us causes us to understand his decrees; it strengthens us and enables us to walk faithfully according to his word.

Ephesians 2:10 NLT

For we are God's masterpiece. He has created us anew in Christ Jesus, so we can do the right things he planned for us long ago.

Been a masterpiece in God implies, our lives have been crafted deliberately before we knew who we are. Each of our steps is chosen not by mere coincidence but out of Gods intentionality.

We are renewed in Christ the moment we choose to be his follower. Anything God does through or with us is to fulfil His purpose for us so that our life can bring him glory.

Having the spirit of God in us means we no longer own ourselves. He directs and orders our steps in the way we ought to go, if only we are obedient allowing his influence. He becomes an obsession when we have found Him worthy of overseeing our lives. We hunger for more of Him.

When we find the truth, which is Jesus, it sets us free from every bondage. Our walk is directed towards his light burden. His love for us brings glory to his name as we reciprocate his love towards humanity if we do not relapse in faith. The more we run towards Him, the More He wants to embrace us, as a Father cuddles in love, compassion, and mercy.

John 8:32 NLT

And you will know the truth, and the truth will set you free."

Matthew 11:28-30 NLT

Then Jesus said, "Come to me, all of you who are weary and carry heavy burdens, and I will give you rest. Take my yoke upon you. Let me teach you, because I am humble and gentle at heart, and you will find rest for your souls. For my yoke is easy to bear, and the burden I give you is light."

God's intent for creating us is that our life will bring glory to His Holy Name in whichever level of Christianity, either as babes or as mature, just as **a piece becomes a masterpiece in the hands of a creator. It cannot be hidden; it will be displayed for the whole world to see for t**he Name of God to be glorified. A displayed masterpiece will showcase the magnificence of the creator's craft, skill and the intelligence applied in creating that piece. In the same way, our life will transform once we submit to his leadership through the help of the Holy Spirit.

John 14:6 NLT

Jesus told him, "I am the way, the truth, and the life. No one can come to the father except through me.

John 6:44 NLT

For no one can come to me unless the father who sent me draws them to me, and on the last day I will raise them up.

We can only manifest the good plans through Jesus Christ, our strength and the revealer of every good plan, the utmost reason we were created and called to His great commission. Jesus Christ is the only way, the only truth, and the only path to getting to the Father. Until we have been forgiven, cleansed, and redeemed, until we have believed in the paid price of redemption, becoming a curse for our sake by dying on the tree, we cannot get to the father. The Father is searching for those who are his and have been foreknown to him. It is always a privilege to be a part of those the Lord sorts for. To God be all the glory.

Lesson 15: Christ Dwells Within.

The rhythm of my life changed, and I knew I could not do things in the same manner as before. I just had the urge to relate differently to my environment. One day in church, all the young adults gathered, and we were asked to pray. Lola had taught me how and why we need to pray as we prayed together often.

It was interesting to know the dimensions one can get to in the spirit that produces positive results. The hunger for prayer never ceased. It escalated as I grew older in the Lord. It is indeed a fact that a spirit dwells in our hearts, He grieves if we do not walk according to the spirit and it is only through consistency in prayer that we can maintain our spiritual walk, and not gratify the desires of the flesh.

In prayer, I realised I could sing. I found peace and contentment whenever I sang. I did not know many gospel songs then, so I would compose my rhythm in my own words.

Singing became my safe place. Anytime I felt rejected, incapable, useless and cheated on, I would resort to singing. I would sing my pain out, cry out and call out the name of the Lord. I found security in my personal worship to God, and it lifts burdens. It remained my "Go to" anytime I worshipped.

Lesson

Ministry does not begin when we receive a title or undergo a form of ordination.

Ministry begins the moment we give our life to Christ.

It starts immediately we accept Jesus Christ as our Lord and personal saviour. From that moment, we become a representation of him on earth, a follower of Jesus. This then result in the need for our hearts to exhibit his intentions. He reaches our hearts by placing circumstances that will influence a change of heart.

We can either align ourselves to his will or decide to remain unchanged. When we allow God to be our ultimate choice, he will show us which path we should take. He will lead us to our destination, which means our ministry has begun.

We cannot accomplish anything without the influence of our creator, nothing can be done without God's intervention. That is why it's paramount to dedicate every day to our creator so that our choices will be Christ-influenced.

Matthew 11:28 NLT

Then Jesus said, "Come to me, all of you who are weary and carry heavy burdens, and I will give you rest.

Jeremiah 33:3 KJV

Call unto me, and I will answer thee, and shew thee great and mighty things, which thou knowest not.

When we call on the Lord, choosing to abide in him and if his words dwell in us, He will show us great and mighty things we have no idea of, destinations we never imagined we could reach and achievements we never thought we could attain by our abilities.

John 15:16 KJV

Ye have not chosen me, but I have chosen you, and ordained you, that ye should go and bring forth fruit, and that your fruit should remain that whatsoever ye shall ask of the Father in my name, he may give it you.

John 15:7 NLT

But if you remain in me and my words remain in you, you may ask for anything you want, and it will be granted!

Romans 8:27-28 NLT

And the Father who knows all hearts knows what the Spirit is saying, for the Spirit pleads for us believers in harmony with God's own will. And we know that God causes everything to work together for the good of those who love God and are called according to his purpose for them.

Philippians 2:12-13 NLT

Dear friends, you always followed my instructions when I was with you. And now that I am away, it is even more important. Work hard to show the results of your salvation, obeying God with deep reverence and fear. For God is working in you, giving you the desire and the power to do what pleases him.

Lesson 16: I Lost My Friend-Sister

There came a time when Lola received the devastating news that her dad had gone to be with Lord. She was very broken and cried most of the time. How I wished I could ease her pain; nothing can ever replace the loss of a loved one. It became necessary that she return to her family, as she needed to be present at her daddy's burial.

As it got closer to her leaving for her hometown, we spoke less to each other. I did not know how to help ease the pain she was in. I was heartbroken my friend was in pain, and I could not help her.

All she could say to me was to continue being a good girl and remember that God loves me. I wished she would stay forever since I knew I would not be able to go to church on my own. Who was going to read the bible to me or pray with me? I just knew my life was not going to be the same again.

The due date for her departure came. We said a tearful goodbye, and she entered the car. I did not think to get any information to trace her, neither do my parents remember which town she came from. My friend was gone forever. I never got to see her again. I pray God's covering on her wherever she is.

How heart-breaking this was! I cried out like a baby anytime her name came to mind. I could not believe that a person I had come to trust and love like my relative was gone and would never come back again. Her last words kept me going, "Continue to be a good girl and know that God loves you".

Lesson

God provides what we need, not what we want. He provides exactly what we need and what we can handle. Just like the days of manna, the children of Israel were asked to pick enough for the day, and any leftovers would go rotten.

People do come and go to fulfil a mandate. The impact they make on us is greatly realised in their absence. We either outgrow their connection, or they become inaccessible.

It can be a positive or negative impact, depending on who they are, what is being impacted and how we have responded to them, which either propel us to our next season or prolong our journey. Impact deemed as negative may be ordained by God for our growth and transformation, just as in Joseph's life through slavery. Remember, all things work together for the good of those who are his and love God. **The enemy's plan may seem to be succeeding for a while, but it will ultimately fail and provide us an opportunity to move forward.**

David referenced how he's killed bears and lions with his bare hands in the wilderness. This gave him confidence that the God who saw him through those difficult times could still uphold him as he faced Goliath.

A positive relationship like what I experienced with Lola is an example of how God uses people to teach and lead us to places of destiny we are unaware was part of our journey until we got there. She came into my life and my home so that I could have a better understanding of what it means to be a Child of God. She did not only lead me to Christ but she was also used as an instrument of light. I saw the light through her. I received the most important foundation for my Christian walk.

John 14:18 NLT

'No, I will not abandon you as orphans—I will come to you. '

Jeremiah 29:11 NLT

'For I know the plans I have for you," says the Lord. "They are plans for good and not for disaster, to give you a future and a hope. '

Romans 8:28 NLT

'And we know that God causes everything to work together for the good of those who love God and are called according to his purpose for them. '

1 Samuel 17:36-37 KJV

"Thy servant slew both the lion and the bear: and this uncircumcised Philistine shall be as one of them, seeing he hath defied the armies of the living God. David said moreover, The Lord that delivered me out of the paw of the lion, and out of the paw of the bear, he will deliver me out of the hand of this Philistine. And Saul said unto David, Go, and the Lord be with thee. '

Lesson 17: Separation Point

There came a turning point in our family when Daddy lost his job as a banker due to the government's legislation on liquidating the National Bank of Nigeria. The staff were rendered jobless. This occurred around 1992. The whole country of Nigeria went on strike, especially government institutions and businesses in response to the liquidation. It was a challenging season for every family in Nigeria.

Daddy had to decide on how to cater for the family. He then converted our family car into a taxi, and he became a taxi driver. I still do not know how he managed to perform well. Undoubtedly, he is a fighter. Nothing on him showed he had ever been a banker or had the experience of a taxi driver, yet he did well. At the end of his day, I counted his money and recorded it in a book. I was his bookkeeper.

Schools were on strike as well, we stayed home for quite a long time waiting for the government to resolve the issues prevailing, yet things never seem to be changing.

Daddy had to decide because there were riots everywhere, and it was becoming unsafe to be anywhere. He decided we would go to Ghana while waiting for the situation in Nigeria to subside, and since we had never been to Ghana, he thought we would use this opportunity to visit. This was in 1992. I was 13 years old, and my sister was eight years old.

Mum didn't come with us because she worked in the Ministry of Health at the time, she didn't want to be away when she was most needed. Another reason was that mom was training for her next promotion, so she stayed to complete it.

The day finally came for the journey. I could not bid my friends goodbye as I thought I would be coming back. I did not know what to expect, but the excitement of seeing Ghana for the first time captivated me.

Lesson

Isaiah 43:1

But now, this is what the LORD says- he who created you, Jacob, he who formed you, Israel: "Do not fear, for I have redeemed you; I have summoned you by name; you are mine.

When life takes a sudden turn, it brings fear and uncertainty. Our decisions emanate from knowledge, insecurities, uncertainties, and experiences. All these have the propensity to influence our outcome. This posture determines the route we end up taking.

Irrespective of our inclination, we can achieve great things by finding the strength that's always inside. It will be inhuman not to fear or wobble when embarking on a great venture. It is a sign of our desire to succeed. This is where faith in God is deemed necessary; even if we don't know what is next, we trust God who knows everything.

Bishop T.D Jakes wrote in his book Crushing that "Now more than ever we must begin seeing that the plans we have imagined for our lives cannot compare to God's strategy for fulfilling our divine purpose". In that, even if we take the wrong turn, which may result in us being crushed, we become like wine in the process, which is usable. Psalm 23:1-6NKJV states his rod and staff comforts me, and it leads me in the path of righteousness for His Name's sake. This is an assurance to us that, out of His love and promise, we will never leave His sight unprotected. He will not leave us as an orphan (John 14: 18-24 NKJV) but will be a shepherd who cares for his sheep.

It is therefore paramount that our pursuit should be to stay connected to the Father who knows the end from the beginning, who formed us, owns us, and knows us by name. He will usher us as we journey with him in trust. Even if we miss our way, his grace is sufficient to bring us back to our destined path, only if we choose to reroute and reconnect when his voice calls, like the prodigal son who returned to himself, Luke 15:17-20KJV.

It is also necessary that before we take any step, we seek the face of God's will and direction in the matter. This requires consistent prayer and discernment to identify the green light before taking a turn in our life journey to prevent the error of missing out on God's timing and his purpose for us. May our merciful God who is faithful see us through. Amen

Isaiah 42:6

I, the LORD, have called you in righteousness; I will take hold of your hand. I will keep you and will make you to be a covenant for the people and a light for the Gentiles,

Psalms 37:23 KJV

'The Lord directs the steps of the godly. He delights in every detail of their lives.'

Psalm 23:1-6 NKJV

The Lord is my shepherd. I shall not want. He makes me to lie down in green pastures. He leads me beside the still waters. He restores my soul. He leads me in the path of righteousness, for His name's sake. Yea, though I walk through the valley of the shadow of death, I will fear no evil. For You are with me. Your rod and Your staff, they comfort me. You prepare a table before me in the presence of my enemies. You anoint my head with oil. My cup runs over. Surely goodness and mercy shall follow me—all the days of my life. And I will dwell in the house of the Lord. Forever.

If we endeavour to make our God our guide, we will not miss our path. Remember, God does not make mistakes, and everything happens for a reason. It's either to teach, build or strengthen us. Rest in his presence, His Love, and His grace knowing that he who has begun a new thing, will bring it to a completion.

Lesson 18: The Journey to Ghana

The Journey to Ghana began as arranged. It was like a journey to the unknown. It was exciting yet scary since my mom was not coming with us. However, seeing my motherland and other family members was quite exciting. The opportunity to experience the stories our parents told us firsthand felt like a dream come true.

It took us two days on the road, with a lot of stops, to eat, use the toilets at filling stations, etc., as we journeyed on to Ghana. There was a lot of sleeping on the bus and it felt like we would never reach our destination.

We finally got to my dad's hometown, Axim, in the western region of Ghana. I got to see other family members including grand aunties. We stayed there for a few months and had the opportunity to get used to the varieties of foods and the native language. We began unlearning old habits and learned new skills as we adapted to the culture.

Months went into years, and the strike back in Nigeria didn't subside. It was then advised that we remained and started schooling. Another change of plan occurred; we were no longer going back. The question is, where was my mom? When was she coming?

The fun came to an end, reality began setting in and we were then treated as any other person. I had to fend for myself, wash my plate, take part in house chores, stand for myself as I related with other kids and cousins and was no longer seen as a visitor but a family member. Even though I was managing to conform, I still didn't feel like I belonged. I felt like an alien around family members. The only person I knew well was my younger sister. I protected her like myself.

We needed to find a place of our own and start schooling which Dad did in Takoradi.

This was the point where I realised that things would not be the same. I embraced the unfamiliarity's and new environment with resilience. I became stronger and adapted to my surroundings.

LESSON

This was not an easy thing for me as I had never lived anywhere outside our home without my parents; none of them were available. We were left in the care of distant grand-aunties, aunties, and cousins. There was also a language barrier because our English was different, especially our accent. Our preference for food was different. Moreover, no one had the time to sit with us and talk about anything. It was a lonely place.

For some reason, I developed the ability to search for my happiness and joy from within. Through self-reflection and a new sense of self-awareness, I could keep out of harm's way. I was quiet and spoke less. I was an observer, making sense of things in my way. It felt like my normal temperament, whereas it was just me not comfortable with this new environment.

As time passed, I developed the character of listening to the voice within. I didn't know what it was, but that voice seemed to give me understanding and the knowing of the things going on around me. It gave me so much satisfaction and contentment that I no longer faced the fear of being alone or afraid. The absence of my parents became less worrying. I learnt to hear the Holy Spirit speak. I remembered a God who lived within us and spoke to us daily, so I found solace in the presence of God within. I was not always perfect but knowing that there is a God was such a relief.

John 15:26-27 NIV

"When the Advocate comes, whom I will send to you from the Father—the Spirit of truth who goes out from the Father—he will testify about me. And

you also must testify, for you have been with me from the beginning.

Our experience with the Lord Jesus never ends. Once we have a touch of His presence, it goes with us wherever we find ourselves. He is the omnipotent and omniscient God whose Love for us never runs dry, and he never departs. When we dig down within ourselves, trusting that He is available, He will make Himself known in ways we never thought possible, for the Lord is closer to us than we can envisage.

Right from the first encounter with Him when I joined other kids to pray in the church I was attending in Nigeria. His presence filled my heart with more of Him than I ever thought needed.

The Holy Spirit is my constant companion, even when the path is unclear. But I was comforted knowing He who watches over Israel never sleeps nor slumber. He is with those who believe and trust in His faithfulness.

Psalms 121:2-8 NIV

My help comes from the Lord, the Maker of heaven and earth. He will not let your foot slip— he who watches over you will not slumber; indeed, he who watches over Israel will neither slumber nor sleep. The Lord watches over you— the Lord is your shade at your right hand; the sun will not harm you by day, nor the moon by night. The Lord will keep you from all harm— he will watch over your life; the Lord will watch over your coming and going both now and forevermore.

He is everywhere with you, so don't be afraid. Just trust Him and draw from His strength, available whenever needed.

Lesson 19: Dependence on God

The strike persisted in Nigeria, which meant we were not going back anytime soon. We then needed to find a permanent place to stay, so we started living with someone we realised was my dad's ex-girlfriend. We couldn't explain the relationship, but we ended up living with her. I registered for school and was placed in year two of Junior Secondary School, equivalent to year 8 in the UK. My expected year mates had already registered for the Basic Education Certificate Exams (BECE) so, I couldn't join that class.

At this point, we were looked after by a stepmum, someone I didn't know existed. Getting to know her and adjusting to this new family was a challenge, considering the confusion of where I was. She had three children, a female house help, and three of us, making six children and two adults in a one-bedroom shared house. We lived in a house where the kitchen and other facilities were shared with other people who were not family members.

Dad was barely around. He went and returned weekly or bi-weekly, depending on how business went for him, as he was trying to build a business that could be a source of income for the entire family.

I was beginning to experience the bitter side of life. There was less food for us and less attention to our basic needs. My body was changing rapidly due to growth, and I didn't understand why, nor did I know what to do. My source of advice was from friends and a few adults who cared to teach me. I would cry, wanting to go back to my mum, but there were no means of talking to her as we didn't have mobile phones back in the 1990s. My only option was to write a letter. Even if I did, posting it was impossible as I didn't have money for food, talk less of posting a letter to Nigeria.

The treatment given to us was different when Dad was around, so whatever I told him regarding the situation at home seemed like a lie and unacceptable. It was as if I was trying to create a problem for myself. I was told to stop complaining so I don't get kicked out.

This was the beginning of my experience with pain and rejection. I was maltreated and felt unloved. They told lies about me and punished me for things I didn't do, I harboured my pain as there was no one to confide in. I faced rejection and I lost confidence to mingle with friends.

This continued for a while, and then people who cared told my dad to do something about the situation. It resulted in a lot of tension at home. My dad finally found a place and we moved out of that place. I took the Basic Education Certificate Exams (BECE), waited for the results to continue to the senior secondary school (SSS).

Lesson

Whenever a season changes, there is a pushing force announcing that you've expired that space. This can come in the form of rejection or an incident that will require you to no longer exist in that environment. It sometimes feels like the enemy's handiwork, but it may be an indication of ending that chapter.

We require prayer for divine strength to journey through the seasons, as we may feel discouraged. **Prayer is buying into and building spiritual capacity for Gods purpose rather than wallowing in pain.** It is for us to guard our hearts and emotions, watching how we respond to the circumstance, not to abort the seed deposited in us because of pain. Praying allows us to discern the correct response, preventing us from moving out too early or too late. It prevents acting out of His will.

When we pray, we acknowledge that God exists and we are dependent on His divine move, just as the Israelites did when they were in slavery in the land of Egypt. They prayed and groaned, waiting for the hand of God to manifest. He finally came when His time of redemption was due.

Exodus 2:23-25 NIV

During that long period, the king of Egypt died. The Israelites groaned in their slavery and cried out, and their cry for help because of their slavery went up to God. God heard their groaning, and he remembered his covenant with Abraham, with Isaac and with Jacob. So, God looked on the Israelites and was concerned about them.

The cry of the Israelites reached out to God, and he decided to do something about it, not forgetting that He already had a plan. Moses had been born purposely for this cause. Moses needed to be of age, with the right character, experience, and exposure for what he'd been purposed or called to do. The Purpose of Moses was to be the deliverer for the Israelites. Moreover, the Israelites thought the Lord had forgotten them and that he was never coming for them. Rather, His time for deliverance was not due in God's calendar.

When the time and season of God is due, He will make His promise happen.

Exodus 3: 7-10 NIV

The LORD said, "I have indeed seen the misery of my people in Egypt. I have heard them crying out because of their slave drivers, and I am concerned about their suffering. So, I have come down to rescue them from the hand of the Egyptians and to bring them up out of that land into a good and spacious land, a land flowing with milk and honey—the home of the Canaanites, Hittites, Amorites, Perizzites, Hivites and Jebusites. And now the cry of the Israelites has reached me, and I have seen the way the Egyptians are oppressing them. So now, go. I am sending you to Pharaoh to bring my people the Israelites out of Egypt."

The Lord never leaves us on our own. He fights, rescues, and saves us from anything holding us bound. He will not allow the enemy's desire to prevail over His chosen one. Even in His silence, He is still working, ensuring victory, and getting glory. By then, you would have attained the character for the new season.

Lesson 20: A New Page Began

Writing the exams and receiving results took six months of waiting. One of my aunties came from Kumasi to visit us in Takoradi, and she decided to take me with her to Kumasi. I was devastated as I was seeing her for the second time in a long time. Considering my previous experience, going to stay with another person was something I was not happy about.

After crying and expressing my dissatisfaction, Dad explained it was the best option as he couldn't take care of us; moreover, he was travelling. It hurt me to know that my sister would live with another auntie. We were going to be separated for the first time since we came.

According to the arrangement, I moved to Kumasi with my auntie and her family. It was quite a modern town and bigger compared to Takoradi.

My auntie and her husband taught me womanhood. They gave me the model of parenthood and a home. It was a new season for unlearning and relearning many things including house chores.

There, I learnt how to care for children, obedience, and discipline. I couldn't just go out without a reason. I learnt to set priorities right and was careful about my decisions.

By this this time, I had gained admission to the Senior Secondary School and had taken the Senior Secondary school exams after three years. My exam results were finally released but it was too weak to gain admission into the university, so I had to rewrite some subjects.

At the remedial school, my accounting teacher requested to meet him in his office. He asked about my previous school and subjects. He asked about my circumstances and why I failed most of my exams. He then advised me to concentrate on my studies to attain the right qualifications for the

40 Lessons in 40 in Years | 131

university. He encouraged me to forget about everything I may have gone through and concentrate on where I was in other to reach my goal for success. **He reiterated that problems do come no matter the stage of life, but if I keep focusing on what could have been rather than what's ahead, I won't be able to attain success.**

He added that I am the best person who can solve my problems because solving a problem begins with the decision to want it solved.

LESSON

God brings people across our path to teach us the virtues needed for our specific assignment. This includes our parents, family members, teachers, friends and even strangers. It is therefore important for us to discern and identify the people in our life and what they represent.

Bear in mind that these people can also be demonic agents aiming to divert our journey in God.

They could come through friendships or negative advice from a person in higher authority.

It is therefore necessary to pray for a discerning spirit that searches all truth to identify the true counsel from God.

In Exodus 18:9-12, Moses' father-in-law Jethro, was also a priest who taught Moses how to delegate roles. He instructed him to select able men who are God-fearing, trustworthy, and hate dishonest gain, to head various offices and have them serve as judges for the people, especially on simple issues. They only came to Moses when an issue required a higher intervention.

Irrespective of Moses's anointing, he lacked the skill of delegation, which is the most important area of leadership. God had to use Jethro, his father-in-law, to teach him that. If Moses had ignored his advice, he would have short-lived his ministry of leading the people of God.

Exodus 18: 14-26 NIV

When his father-in-law saw all that Moses was doing for the people, he said, "What is this you are doing for the people? Why do you alone sit as judge, while all these people stand around you from morning till evening?"

Moses answered him, "Because the people come to me to seek God's will. Whenever they have a dispute, it is brought to me, and I decide between the parties and inform them of God's decrees and instructions."

Moses' father-in-law replied, "What you are doing is not good. You and these people who come to you will only wear yourselves out. The work is too heavy for you; you cannot handle it alone. Listen now to me and I will give you some advice, and may God be with you. You must be the people's representative before God and bring their disputes to him. Teach them his decrees and instructions and show them the way they are to live and how they are to behave. But select capable men from all the people—men who fear God, trustworthy men who hate dishonest gain—and appoint them as officials over thousands, hundreds, fifties, and tens. Have them always serve as judges for the people but have them bring every difficult case to you; the simple cases they can decide themselves. That will make your load lighter because they will share it with you. If you do this and God so commands, you will be able to stand the strain, and all these people will go home satisfied."

Moses listened to his father-in-law and did everything he said. He chose capable men from all Israel and made them leaders of the people, officials over thousands, hundreds, fifties, and tens. They always served as judges for the people. The difficult cases they brought to Moses, but the simple ones they decided themselves.

In the book of Judges 16, Samson was persuaded to reveal the secret of the source of his strength to someone he trusted so well and loved.

Delilah betrayed that trust because she realised that Samson was in love with her and would do anything for her happiness. **She thrived on his emotions to betray him.** This relationship led to Samson's downfall. He lost his power, his eyesight and the presence of God left him. Losing his hair meant losing the source of his strength.

As much as Samson was able to retaliate against the Philistines when his hair grew back, he lost his life along with destroying the Philistines. He could have fulfilled his assignment without dying if not for the wrong company. Therefore, we ought to consciously have people on the same journey as us who believe in the same Godly principles as we do. **We must be careful of where we seek advice when we are emotionally imbalanced, so we don't derail our journey.**

Judges 16: 15-17, 21,22 NKJV

Then she said to him, "How can you say, 'I love you,' when you won't confide in me? This is the third time you have made a fool of me and haven't told me the secret of your great strength." With such nagging she prodded him day after day until he was sick to death of it.

So, he told her everything. "No razor has ever been used on my head," he said, "because I have been a Nazirite dedicated to God from my mother's womb. If my head were shaved, my strength would leave me, and I would become as weak as any other man."

After putting him to sleep on her lap, she called for someone to shave off the seven braids of his hair, and so began to subdue him. And his strength left him.

Then the Philistines seized him, gouged out his eyes and took him down to Gaza. Binding him with bronze shackles, they set him to grinding grain in the prison. But the hair on his head began to grow again after it had been shaved.

Judges 16: 28-30

Then Samson prayed to the LORD, "Sovereign LORD, remember me. Please, God, strengthen me just once more, and let me with one blow get revenge on the Philistines for my two eyes." Then Samson reached toward the two central pillars on which the temple stood. Bracing himself against them, his right hand on the one and his left hand on the other, Samson said, "Let me die with the Philistines!" Then he pushed with all his might, and down came the temple on the rulers and all the people in it. Thus, he killed many more when he died than while he lived.

In conclusion, 1 Peter 5:8 admonishes us to be vigilant because the roaring lion, the devil, consistently looks for who to devour. He uses various devices, so we ought to be cautious of our decisions and choices, as we trust in the will and process of God to get to our purposed destination. **Be on the watch.**

1 Peter 5:8-9 NKJV

Be sober, be vigilant; because your adversary the devil walks about like a roaring lion, seeking whom he may devour. Resist him, steadfast in the faith, knowing that the same sufferings are experienced by your brotherhood in the world.

CHAPTER 3: THE LORD SAW ME

Lesson 21: Stepping into Ministry

A friend who lived close to our house in Kumasi invited me to her church. She wanted me to meet her pen pal, someone she'd been exchanging letters with. She was so excited about their friendship that she desperately wanted me to see this guy by visiting their church. The guy was one of the young pastors who interpreted for the Pastor.

I asked permission to go with their family to church. It was my first time going anywhere on my own, which was an opportunity for me to see other places.

Entering the church, I felt the presence of God, something like a weight of glory, which I gravitated towards, and I wanted to remain there. As we settled down and the service progressed into choir ministration, my desire to join them was palpable.

My friend showed me this guy and how funny he was, she couldn't stop laughing. Everything the guy said was amusing to her. As much as I could identify his gift, I thought my friend was not listening to the preacher. She was just fascinated with this guy.

All I thought about was how to become a member of this church and join the choir. My auntie and husband are Catholic, I wasn't sure I would be allowed to attend a different church talk of joining the choir.

As time passed, I became a full member of the church, Family Chapel International, located on Susanso Road, Kumasi-Ghana. I went till I joined the choir.

My first day of rehearsals was not enjoyable as I was unfamiliar with the songs. I was happy I joined as it felt like a new venture. Even though choir members were not very friendly as they had made their own friends. I gradually immersed in the group.

When I listen to gospel songs, they minister to my soul. Gospel music became my safe space, where I could pour out my heart, knowing that I wasn't just singing but offering my worship to God. It connected me to the love of God.

I have tasted God's love; therefore, I want to continuously dwell in it. The first time I heard him speak audibly to me was in worship. I identify with who He made me in worship.

LESSON

There is always a meeting point with God. Especially when the Lord is drawing you closer to himself. He walks you through seasons of seclusion or rejection. It suddenly feels like people who used to love you, begins to find something wrong with you. **The safest place anyone can be is the presence of God.**

Paul in the Bible hated and killed believers, but when his season of transformation was due, he became blind to his past in exchange for an encounter with God. This resulted in his total conversion to what he disapproved of. That encounter with the Lord transformed him so much that he found his true purpose, and the name he answered to changed from Saul to Paul.

Acts 22: 6-7,10-11 TPT

As I was on the road approaching Damascus, about noon, a brilliant heavenly light suddenly appeared, flashing all around me. As I fell to the ground, I heard a voice say, 'Saul, Saul . . . why are you persecuting me?'

"So, I asked, 'Lord, what am I to do?'

"And the Lord said to me, 'Get up and go into Damascus, and there you will be told about all that you are destined to do.'

"Because of the dazzling glory of the light, I couldn't see—I was left blind. So, they had to lead me by the hand the rest of the way into Damascus.

Genesis 16:7-8 ESV, 13NIV

The angel of the LORD found her by a spring of water in the wilderness, the spring on the way to Shur. And he said, "Hagar, maid of Sarai, where have you come from and where are you going?" She said, "I am fleeing from my mistress Sarai.

She gave this name to the Lord who spoke to her: "You are the God who sees me," for she said, "I have now seen the One who sees me.

Hagar was in the wilderness by the spring of water when she encountered the angel of the Lord, which brought her to repentance in character and how she behaved towards her master, Sarai. There is always a point of encounter where repentance is inevitable.

Lesson 22: Look Within

My relationship with the church began to bud. I felt content in a moment and out of place the next. I struggled to identify myself, and I could not fully fit into anything. I lived fearfully and withdrawn from life. I felt defenceless, and the fear of the unknown crippled me. Confidence was not in my confessions, yet I managed to enter a relationship.

I met a guy in my secondary school days. He was ahead of me educationally and highly intelligent, which I drew towards. I believed in his judgement, which resulted in his controlling character. I did not know who I was anyway, so it was unnecessary to counteract, as I trusted in his judgements.

Not that his suggestions were evil per se, or they led me into any vices, but they were from his fear. He was controlling and I had to explain everything. There was no trust in the relationship whatsoever, we were constantly arguing.

Even though he taught me simple skills, like how to dress, what to wear and not to, the style of clothes for my body type, etc. I was only fortunate his influences were not vices or substance misuse.

Lesson

An identity crisis is a period of uncertainty in which a person's sense of identity becomes insecure, typically due to a change in their expected aims or role in society. This can also be due to an unhealthy environment where identity is demeaned, where incapabilities are constantly spoken about rather than encouraging abilities. An abusive environment that degrades and devalues one's identity results in getting attached to things that give either stimulation or some form of assurance.

As we grow up, our identity evolves along with major life changes. A teenagers priority differs from a matured adult. Priority changes for a woman who becomes a mother or wife compared to a young college student. Therefore, it is possible to identify with things that gives a sense of importance. People may tie their importance to their children, work, and achievements. Others may prefer substance abuse such as drugs, alcohol, or certain people to satisfy inclusion.

All these will continue if we cannot find an ultimate satisfaction that can speak positivity into our lives, which influences our thought process to identify our identity even if we lose it along the line.

1 Corinthians 6:12 Amp

Everything is permissible for me, but not all things are beneficial. Everything is permissible for me, but I will not be enslaved by anything [and brought under its power, allowing it to control me].

Knowing who we are can only be found in Christ, as he created us, breathed life into our lungs and called us His own. If we are His, He is aware of our identity and everything pertaining to life. Therefore, the best place to know who we are is to surrender our life to God, walking righteously and faithfully in Him. Then, He begins to show us who He made us and His intention for us, which is our purpose.

1 Corinthians 6: 12Amp version clearly states that, anything that controls or has power over us has us enslaved to His power and influence. Apostle Paul explains further that as much as all things are permissible, not all benefits the child of God. This means the things we allow can either have us enslaved or delivered.

1 John 2:17Amp

The world is passing away, and with it its lusts [the shameful pursuits and ungodly longings]; but the one who does the will of God and carries out His purpose lives forever.

It is the will of God that you walk with Him in obedience and in righteousness as he shows you the way and helps you find your identity in Christ. **To be delivered, is to be freed from the power of what we have been delivered from.**

Lesson 23: Mercy In God

As I began indulging in the things of God, being a part of the choir was the best decision ever. My relationship became intimate, and my trust in His sovereignty began solidifying. My spirit was always awakened to the knowing that He Loves me irrespective.

Church became a second home. Not only did it draw me close to God, but it also prevented me from indulging in social vices. I was gradually losing interest in the ungodly things I was involved in.

I was in a relationship with a university student who was one of the executive leaders of the university. We met when He was in his second year and I was in my final year of secondary school. By the 4th year of our relationship, I had gained admission into the Kumasi Polytechnic, studying for a Diploma in Business Studies. I was preparing to resit my SSCE (senior secondary certificate exams) as I needed to pass six subjects for the university compared to four passes for a diploma.

It got to a point where I felt out of place as I couldn't fully define myself around him. I had low self-esteem and couldn't mingle much when his friends came around. It felt like a weight each time I thought of us. I tried doing things that would anger him and cause him to end the relationship, but he never gave up. It affected how we related, he was afraid of I will end the relationship, and he did everything possible to maintain it.

During this time, he also gained admission for his master's degree in the U.K., but his dad would not fund it. His dad clarified that if he is old enough to have a girlfriend, he should be able to pay for his tuition abroad. Knowing I was the cause of his inability to study abroad scared me away. I couldn't put my feelings into words for his understanding. I just wanted the relationship to end so he could have his freedom. Moreover, I wanted to begin a clean sheet with God. I wanted God to give me what He wanted me to have. I surrendered my desires, asking Him to take over.

Walking away was scary. I walked away broken, but I knew it was necessary. I was convinced if we were meant to be, we would eventually. By then, I would have discovered who I am and can give back to the relationship fully instead of partially.

Lesson

Walking with God requires total surrender, allowing Him to take full charge of our lives by following His precepts daily.

Anytime we release something of importance, it becomes a sacrifice which signifies our trust and total dependence on God. The Lord honours such a sacrifice and blesses us in ways we can't fathom. **Remember, we can never outgive our God.**

Sacrifice means giving to God whatever he requires of us, our time, our earthly possessions and our energies or anything of importance we put away to further His work. When we are willing to sacrifice, it indicates our devotion to God.

Mathew 6: 33Amp

But first and most importantly seek (aim at, strive after) His kingdom and His righteousness [His way of doing and being right—the attitude and character of God], and all these things will be given to you also.

Everything we desire will be available if we learn to let go of the things, we tie importance to more than our Lord.

Lesson 24: Encountering God for Myself

The desire to get closer to God became stronger by the day. It was an unexplainable yearning for me. I spent most of my time reading the Bible and praying, even though I barely understood what I read. However, it was such a delight for me to read the scriptures.

I would listen to worship songs, pray often, and listen to CDs of preachers such as Bishop TD Jakes. My favourite was Prophetess Dr Juanita Bynum. I see myself in her, and I desired to be a gospel singer who can preach the word of God. Her word ministrations were my cup of tea.

I was listening to one of her sermons, and then I began praying and worshipping along, and the presence of God took charge. I didn't know what it was, but I began speaking in a different tongue, different from my usual. I laid down on the floor for quite a while speaking in tongues. It was an experience I couldn't explain much, but I knew from then that something divine had taken place in my life. This was my first encounter with Him, and it was marvellous to know that the Lord would make Himself known to a person like me.

Lesson

Having an encounter with God opens the door to a relationship with Him and affirms His presence.

To have an encounter is to experience God intrinsically, and it is distinctive from person to person, depending on their calling, personality, and background.

These are not the basis for experiencing an encounter, they are just the different ways people receive or respond to His presence.

Encountering God is a form of introduction to the person of the Holy Spirit. Knowing the Holy

Spirit as a personality. To love and be transformed by gaining the power to overcome the enemy, breaking the chains of limitation and to be liberated from every ungodly thing in other to be like Him, Sanctified.

Our expression during His visitation can be a form of an emotional expression, i.e., laughing, crying, or feeling a weight all around us. It can also be something unusual happening physically. His presence is felt anytime He wants to make himself known, and we can understand that something special has occurred.

Exodus 3:1-4 NIV

Now Moses was tending the flock of Jethro his father-in-law, the priest of Midian, and he led the flock to the far side of the wilderness and came to Horeb, the mountain of God. There the angel of the LORD appeared to him in flames of fire from within a bush. Moses saw that though the bush was on fire it did not burn up. So, Moses' thought, "I will go over and see this strange sight—why the bush does not burn up." When the LORD *saw that he had gone over to look, God called to him from within the bush, "Moses! Moses! "And Moses said, "Here I am."*

Seeing an unusual burning bush drew Moses's attention, prompting him to look closer. When his attention turned to see the burning bush, God began to speak to Him. As much as he wasn't emotional (scripture didn't say), he couldn't deny the divine sight. The presence of God can be clearly identified in an unusual manner. His magnificence can present himself in situations to gain our attention. **He comes down to our level of comprehension yet sacred.**

Acts 2:1-4 NKJV.

When the Day of Pentecost had fully come, they were all with one accord in one place. And suddenly there came a sound from heaven, as of a rushing mighty wind, and it filled the whole house where they were sitting. Then there appeared to them divided tongues, as of fire, and one sat upon each of them. And they were all filled with the Holy Spirit and began to speak with other tongues, as the Spirit gave them utterance.

The disciples experienced the Holy Spirit differently. They had the presence coming like a rushing wind, filling their room. There were divided tongues as of fire which rested on them. **They received not only the Holy Spirit but the capacity to speak in different tongues** that were meaningful to those watching the occurrence, as the Spirit gave them utterance. They also received the power to propagate the gospel as led by the Holy Spirit.

This encounter turned the disciples into another men, they progressed to become Apostles with power.

Mark 16: 15-17NIV

He said to them, "Go into all the world and preach the gospel to all creation. Whoever believes and is baptised will be saved, but whoever does not believe will be condemned. And these signs will accompany those who believe: In my name they will drive out demons; they will speak in new tongues.

Having an encounter is one of the best experiences any child of God can have, as it affirms His love for us, and we are empowered for His work. Encounters bring transformation and are filled with Joy. **God is not limited to a location, He can meet us anywhere based on His choice**, but by the time He reveals Himself to us, our life will never remain the same, as we would have become another person in Christ.

Lesson 25: First Deliverance

I outrightly believed in the things I saw in church, some of which were people falling under the anointing when prayed for. I wanted to experience it by testing my faith to be delivered.

I was bound to masturbation and wanted to be delivered from its power. I wanted to break free from every bondage as I journeyed righteously in God.

The desire arose whenever I saw my nakedness in the mirror. I was in love with myself. It was my safe space, as trusting others was an issue. I would not let anyone come into my space because I was content and comfortable being by myself. I did this to the extent that it affected my romantic relationships. I was unable to respond sexually to my boyfriend since I was content touching myself rather than being with someone. It created an insecurity for him, and he feared losing me to someone else. I was between 21-23 years then. I was independent and content with my space.

Self-absorbing is interest in self, resulting to isolation. The enemy uses this weapon of isolation to contradict Gods intent for Family life, community, by relegating the need for people and God.

Deliverance became necessary as I was not only sinning, but I had not made space for the Holy Spirit to have full control of me. I was self-dependent and lorded over myself. This is referred to Idolatry.

Lesson

Deliverance begins when we accept the need to be set free and the willingness to go through healing process. Otherwise, **deliverance is not complete if we don't accept our infirmity.**

I had seen how people would fall under the anointing when being prayed for. I wanted to get healed too but I couldn't tell anyone about my challenge, so I decided to start praying about it myself.

One day, I stood in front of the mirror after a shower, as usual, and then I began speaking in tongues (language of the spirit). I had a bottle of anointing oil which had been prayed on in one of our church meetings. I poured some on my hand, then I laid my hand on my head in faith. I prayed silently that Father, just as the anointing worked for those I have seen delivered in church, let that same anointing work on me and deliver me from this bondage. I want them no more; I want the Holy Spirit to take full charge of my life in Jesus' Name. I did not see what happened again till I woke up on the other side of the bed. I knew from then that I was delivered, that something had left me.

I recognised that this addiction could not journey with me, and it was necessary to let it go to create space for the Lord to mould me. It was my willingness to let go and the faith that I could be set free which allowed the power of God to deliver me.

Naaman was a ruler and a powerful, influential man, but he suffered from leprosy. This was an unclean disease which does not fit a man of his calibre. Irrespective of the shame attached to this disease, he was willing to do everything for his healing, to the extent that the advice from his maidservant sounded good to him if he wants to be delivered. **He surrendered to the cost of deliverance and got healed.**

2 Kings 5:1 AMP

Naaman, commander of the army of the king of Aram (Syria), was considered a great man by his king, and was highly respected because through Naaman the LORD had given victory to Aram (Syria). He was also a man of courage, but he was a leper.

2 Kings 5:9-11 Amp

So Naaman came with his horses and chariots and stopped at the entrance of Elisha's house. Elisha sent a messenger to him, saying, "Go and wash in the Jordan seven times, and your flesh will be restored to you, and you will be clean." But Naaman was furious and went away and said, "Indeed! I thought 'He would at least come out to [see] me and stand and call on the name of the LORD his God and wave his hand over the place [of leprosy] and heal the leper.'

Sometimes, the enemy will battle with your mind by giving you a reason to forfeit your healing process. Some of these may be the thought of what people will say, not trusting anyone or any other opinion especially if the infirmity seems shameful.

Naaman succumbed to the instructions that will lead to his healing.

2 Kings 5: 13-14 Amp

Then his servants approached and said to him, "My father, if the prophet had told you to do some great thing, would you not have done it? How much more then when he has said to you, 'Wash, and be clean?'" So, he went down and plunged himself into the Jordan seven times, just as the man of God had said; and his flesh was restored like that of a little child, and he was clean.

As much as deliverance occurs supernaturally, we have a part to play. We need God's healing power and the willingness to be made whole, especially when dealing with a shameful addiction. We must be willing to pay the price of discomfort.

Lesson 26: The Struggle for the University Admission

Gaining admission into the university was becoming a challenge as I couldn't attain the pass mark at the first remedial, so I had to do it again. I also needed to get a job while waiting for the results.

Gaining admission was slim as I had three different result slips, which is a sign of weak performance, affecting my chances of attaining the desired course, Business Administration (Banking and Finance).

It dawned on me that without any leverage, my dreams of attaining a degree will die off. I was 24 years of age and had worked in various companies, but because I didn't have a higher qualification, I couldn't progress. I believed I could do better, but the question was how?

In my quest to upgrade myself, I was constantly applying to universities which taught the course I wanted to pursue, but I had been rejected. Prayer and fasting became my only option, that an unusual door would open, that every limitation would be broken and anything that stood in my way of progress would not succeed. I prayed this consistently, everywhere, night and day.

One day after work, I came across a classmate. In a conversation, she told me about a new university established about a year prior, and they were admitting students. It was a newly established university belonging to the Presbyterian Church of Ghana. She explained that matriculation was in one week, bearing in mind that there is no admission after matriculation. I had not checked with my mum if she would be able to afford the tuition, including pocket money but I pursued it in faith.

The miracle began when she confirmed she could afford the required entry fees. A few days after that, the school called to confirm I had been admitted into the course of my choice, and all I needed to do was to be in school within the next three days.

Everything fell into place which I least thought was possible. I went through the admission process, and I was ready for matriculation.

Lesson

Psalm 37:4NLT

Take delight in the LORD and he will give you the desires of your heart.

Whenever we make God the ultimate, He makes us His ultimate. As we walk in His delight, our desires are channelled towards His purpose for us. Even when our desire is outside of His plans, He has a way of turning all things into our good.

Romans 8:28NLT

And we know that God causes everything to work together for the good of those who love God and are called according to his purpose for them.

For those who love the Lord, all things work for our good. All things may not appear good, but we have an advocate who works in our favour.

I never gave up on my desire, nor did I sit wallowing in self-pity because I had no leverage. I was convinced that I would rise beyond every limitation. I was constantly praying about it, believing that God could do it, and He faithfully did.

Lesson 27: Studies and Exams

The beginning of the first semester was rough, as my schoolmates had been in school for about one and a half months before I gained admission. Due to that, I had missed some lecture hours, considering that I entered as a mature working student. The subjects were new to me. Assimilation was challenging, so I had to do more to catch up academically.

As time passed, I joined the existing charismatic movement who were propagating the gospel through music; since the school is a Presbyterian establishment, we ministered in songs in various spiritual gatherings.

I was involved in building the ministry by committing to various meetings and rehearsals, which took much of my time, leaving me with less time to study.

There were times I would pray over my head for understanding and assimilation. I would ask the Lord to show me the areas I need to concentrate on in preparation for the exams, and the Holy Spirit would do exactly so.

In one of my third-year exams, there was a question that involved diagrams and labelling. It comes with twenty marks. We were expected to answer three questions, making sixty marks in all. I did my best with two questions; I was left with one to meet the required three questions. I learnt it, but I couldn't recollect it entirely. Sitting there wandering in thoughts, I prayed that the Holy Spirit would remind me. A few seconds later, I saw the textbook open in the spirit realm. I wrote the answers straight from the opened book. I was amazed at what God had done and my heart was full of gratitude for His divine intervention.

Exams after exams, God proved to be a helper. My GPA increased from 3rd class in year two to 2nd class upper by graduation. This taught me that God is indeed with those who trust Him.

Lesson

As I walk with God, I know God to be a giver. If we ask Him, He gives according to His will. There are times He freely gives even when we don't deserve it, and there are times we ought to ask what we need. It gives us the assurance of His love, faithful judgements, and His Lordship over us.

When we are consistent in the word of God, we are spiritually enlightened. We attain the gift of knowledge, wisdom and understanding. **Consistency in the word of God, causes us to pray according to His will.**

3 John 1:2 AMP

Beloved, I pray that in every way you may succeed and prosper and be in good health [physically], just as [I know] your soul prospers [spiritually].

It is always His desire that we prosper in all things as we aim to please him. He promised to contend with the enemy's contentions because of His love, and to shield us when we go through any challenge, so He gets the glory at the end.

Hosea 4:6KJV

My people are destroyed for lack of knowledge: because thou hast rejected knowledge, I will also reject thee, that thou shalt be no priest to me: seeing thou hast forgotten the law of thy God, I will also forget thy children.

According to the text above, not seeking knowledge or disregarding Gods precepts leads to destruction. **When a child of God chooses the will of God in a matter, it's evidence of submission and obedience to His Lordship.**

Understanding my authority as a child of God, I prayed over my head, declaring retentive memory and divine assistance any time am studying or writing an exam.

This is one of my testimonies, **that all things are possible with God if only we allow Him to interfere with our thoughts.**

Lesson 28: Ministry in School

School life was enjoyable. We were spreading the gospel through music. Our group was called worship warriors and the charismatic choir. We ministered in various school programmes.

Being in the choir continued what I was doing at home. The things of God gave me pleasure, allowing me to connect with God continually. I have never looked back, irrespective of my faults and mishaps. **As I journey, I've found that every step has pushed me forward, regardless of how I stumbled.** Doing what I believe is my calling, growing in wisdom and knowledge of Him with every passing day and season, is a blessing. I deem it a privilege to be part of His grace in the vineyard of the called.

Lesson

Wherever we find ourselves, we emanate the light of God within us. As we proclaim the gospel, it will be incomplete for us not to radiate light, as He is the light called out of darkness.

Samuel was handed over to the priest (Eli) by his mother, Hannah, to fulfil her vow to God if she was given a son. In that same environment, Eli's children were growing wayward, to the extent that it angered God so much that he vowed to take the priesthood off the family of Eli. That same environment allowed Samuel to grow and develop into who he's been called to become, a priest and prophet.

Environments are like the stage God provides for the called to express or fulfil their roles according to God's plans and purposes. It is also where we build, learn, adapt, and cultivate our purpose and calling. The things God allowed me to do in school were a revelation and an indication of my destination. As much as I didn't see it as so, I was just content doing what pleased God, and it kept me on guard.

1 Samuel 1:27-28 NKJV

For this child I prayed; and the LORD *hath given me my petition which I asked of him: Therefore, also I have lent him to the LORD if he liveth he shall be lent to the* LORD. *And he worshipped the* LORD *there.*

1 Samuel 2: 17-18 NKJV

Wherefore the sin of the young men was very great before the Lord: for men abhorred the offering of the Lord. But Samuel ministered before the Lord, being a child, girded with a linen ephod.

Everywhere we go or find ourselves, there is always that part of us that will expose our affiliation with Christ, depicting us as Sons of God. **It is impossible to walk with God and be hidden.**

1 Samuel 2: 14 NKJV

"You are the light of the world. A town built on a hill cannot be hidden.

Lesson 29: Hunger for Prayer

The hunger to pray engulfed me so much that it became my norm. I prayed everywhere I was, night and day, even at work. Random conversations were a distraction to me as I was constantly in prayer. I enjoyed prayer gatherings.

The spirit of prayer helped me go through seasons of uncertainties and confusion, which led to the stillness of my spirit. I cultivated the character of prayer; my choices were prayerfully considered before proceeding.

I identified that my journey and success in life were dependent on the path God created for me, and I was determined in my heart to attain each one of them.

In no time, many victories were won, I saw limitations breaking, and unusual things began to pave the way for me, even at work.

Even when I got employed and promotion didn't seem forth coming as there were more experienced people than me. But I relied on the fact that God had already announced my season of progression.

I didn't allow my inexperience to prevent me from contending in prayer against limitations and disappointment. By the time the interview was due, two people had dropped out, and I finally got promoted. This, among others, encouraged me to pray, knowing that it's the master key to all doors.

There are battles to be won, and there are doors that won't just open unless we stand in prayer. Dwell on the power of God that can break through every limitation into victory.

Lesson

Luke 18:1 NKJV

Then He spoke a parable to them, that men always ought to pray and not lose heart.

Prayer is the engine that drives focus and direction. We pray not only to build our relationship with God but to confirm our need for His strength, as we are weak and nothing without him. Prayer builds focus because it disciplines the flesh. It's a sign of total surrender to His sovereignty.

Lesson 30: The Wedding

Coming back home for the school holiday, I was in my second year at the university. I went for rehearsals on a Saturday in preparation for Sunday choir ministration.

I was late for rehearsals, so as a punishment, I was asked to go on the stage and pray while the rest were watching. After standing there for a few minutes, I was called back to sit with the rest.

As I was walking and looking for a space to sit, there was an empty chair close to someone I had not seen at rehearsals since joining the choir. I had left for school just after my probation, so it was my first time seeing most people at rehearsals.

I sat beside this gentleman, who said hello as I was sitting. I responded hello and smiled. We conversed for a while then exchanged phone numbers. Our journey of friendship began, and it turned into lovers. After about a year and a half, he travelled to the UK, joining His parents and siblings.

As happy as I was for him, I was concerned about our next phase, which engineered my prayer life to another dimension, enquiring from God if this relationship was His will.

We discussed marriage and his plans for our relationship. Everything went as planned. We got engaged on the 15th of January 2011 and had our wedding on 17th July 2011.

I married my friend. We shared the same faith. We were under the same spiritual covering, which I believed was huge. However, there was a part of me that was scared and uncertain. I couldn't define it and couldn't put my feelings into words, talk less of seeking counsel. Here I was in the silence of my fears. I didn't trust my thoughts yet, I went ahead believing that my God, who knows the beginning from the end will intervene.

Lesson

I desired and prayed for someone who loves the Lord. **A partner, who has similar vision in other for us to complement our individual purpose, which is key to the health of the marriage and the upbringing of the children.** That is also what scripture admonishes.

We are all not perfect, there will be some disagreement and agreements. This is how couples build a healthy relationship.

Prayer for my marriage was something I paid attention to. It was consistent and intentional as I understood that marriage exposes the intent of the heart. It can break you up if handled carelessly. As I trusted that the Lord would lead me in making the right choice, I also believed that because of His Fatherly love, I would not be led astray. I believe He intervened, and I went just in the right direction. I held on to the scripture that says, the steps of the righteous are ordered by the Lord.

2 Corinthians 4:16NIV

Do not be yoked together with unbelievers. For what do righteousness and wickedness have in common? Or what fellowship can light have with darkness?

Psalm 37:23-24 NKJV

The steps of a good man are ordered by the LORD, And He delights in his way. Though he falls, he shall not be utterly cast down; For the LORD upholds him with His hand.

CHAPTER 4: SELF ACTUALISATION

Lesson 31: My Journey to the UK

After the wedding celebration, the arrangement was for me to join my husband soon after the wedding. The Lord was gracious unto us, my traveling application was successful. My husband was due to return to UK as he only came to Ghana for our wedding.

We notified our spiritual father, Bishop Dr Victor Osei of our travelling dates, he prayed for us and requested that I come to church on my last Sunday before going, as my husband will be taking the lead to the UK.

On this Sunday, while our pastor was preaching, I heard the Holy Spirit telling me to get up, take off my shoes and put a seed into the offering bowl on the altar as the preaching went on. As I dropped the seed offering in the offering bowl, bishop paused preaching and asked me to get my shoes and place them on my head. I began trembling under the anointing while the shoes were still on my head. Right there, he began declaring in prayers. Some of what he said were: London will favour me, and I will not walk in the streets of London in shame. I fell under the anointing.

I held on to this declaration in faith, an assurance that my journey was divinely influenced and that my steps have been ordered by God as I travelled.

In between planning and preparing to travel, I realised that I was pregnant. The reality of a wife and mother began settling in. I was in more of a hurry to join my husband at this point. The news of pregnancy did not sit well with my husband as he thought there should be a proper laid down plan for a new addition. According to him, the timing was not conducive.

We both concluded that it had already happened. Therefore, we better allow God to take charge of the situation.

Throughout my journey, the fear of the unknown surfaced. How I was going to survive being a wife, mother and transition to an unknown country was altogether very scary for me. I held on to my faith, the spoken word by my spiritual father over my life and the belief that His faithfulness would lead the way.

Lesson

His love for us causes Him to retain the details of our journey so that we do not fear and quit on hope before getting to the finishing point. **As much as he does not give us the full breakdown of our expectations, he leaves fragments and glimpses of what will happen in our journey.** These uncertainties will lead us to pray and enquire for direction. He may also choose to show what is going to happen at the end but leave out the in-between, that's what makes Him God. He knows the end from the beginning and is a father who loves His children so much that He will rather prepare us before giving us the full dosage of his plan. He is such a good, faithful, and dependable God.

On this transitioning journey to the UK, all I had with me was a seed in my womb, one suitcase, trust in God's faithfulness, my spiritual fathers' declarations, and my references of how God has been good before I got to this point.

Remember, the devil will do anything to challenge his stake in a territory or situation. He will always want to interrupt God's agenda to make it look like you have chosen wrongly, but when we hold on to the Lord's word, we will weather the storm and get to our destination safely.

Jeremiah 29:11-13 NKJV

For I know the thoughts that I think toward you, says the LORD, thoughts of peace and not of evil, to give you a future and a hope. Then you will call upon Me and go and pray to Me, and I will listen to you. And you will seek Me and find Me when you search for Me with all your heart.

Lesson 32: Finding My Bearing

Arriving in London in mid-September was exciting but very cold. I met friends I had heard of but had never seen. It was very pleasant to meet everyone. We drove from Heathrow Airport to Toothing Broadway in the Southwest of London, where we lived.

It was a Wednesday, and my husband had to go to church. I could not go with him as I was tired and needed rest after about a day's journey. Waking up from my rest, I decided to walk around the area to know my surroundings.

As I walked about, I began praying, taking charge of the land, repeating what had already been declared by my spiritual father. Declaring that it would bring me and my seeds favour and provision I declared that this land would not bring me shame. Despite the uncertainties, I believed my God would see me through, and I would see the good of the Lord in the Land of the Living.

I walked around every evening, while trying to exercise my body and to gain the understanding of where everything was, including finding an African shop in the area, which helped with my cravings.

Lesson

The Lord is gracious unto those he calls chosen, those he chose and foreknew before they were born and even before they knew Him. He is interested in our challenges, weaknesses, and uncertainties. To understand spiritual things will require getting into the spirit, but there is always the tendency of us trying to get an understanding through the flesh. He is the alpha and the omega; he knows the end from the start. **Therefore, everything He unveils as we journey with Him in faith has the end inclusive.**

We cannot hide from the Lord in any way, not in our emotions. We cannot pretend we have it all, whereas the posture of our heart does not match our expression. **When the Lord takes the lead in our life, He reorders everything including our path and appetite. These influence our choices.**

Zephaniah 3:16-17 NKJV

On that day they will say to Jerusalem: "Do not fear, O Zion; do not let your hands fall limp. The LORD your God is among you; He is mighty to save. He will rejoice over you with gladness; He will quiet you with His love; He will rejoice over you with singing."

Psalm 23: 3-4NIV

He restores my soul; He guides me in the paths of righteousness for the sake of His name. Even though I walk through the valley of the shadow of death, I will fear no evil, for You are with me; Your rod and Your staff, they comfort me.

Lesson 33: Living with my In-law.

As I approached my due date, we agreed I would move to my in-laws for support when the baby arrived. I needed to start gathering baby essentials however, I had no clue what those essentials were. Considering our financial circumstances, I needed to be wise with my spending. I was worried about my health and that of the baby. I wondered if I was going to be a good mother because I had no clue about motherhood.

I couldn't eat much and was constantly vomiting. I was afraid my baby wasn't getting the right amount of nutrients. Thank God for mothers. My mum navigated each stage with me, exploring what works and educating me on pregnancy normalities.

Going to live with my in-laws was a life-saving solution. I got to understand their family culture and values, which was different from mine. I understood my husband better, as some of his responses were due to his background.

Here, I learnt new skills as a mother, including the British way of life. I had to learn the simplest things, such as the clothing for each season. I understood that babies grow so quickly therefore, it was unnecessary to buy excessive baby clothing. This understanding released me from the pressure of unnecessary baby needs. I understood that the most important necessity is food, appropriate clothes for the season, many nappies in each size, and the strength and energy to care for the growing baby, who demands more attention than anything else. The greatest part is everyone in the family was excited about the new arrival.

In anticipation, there was a little hiccup in our everyday planning- agreeing with the various opinions—my opinion as a mother, my biological mother as a medical practitioner and my in-law. There were contradictions to what Mum says from a medical viewpoint to tradition. This sometimes-caused heightened emotional breakdown while trying to be polite, understanding and voicing my preference.

My only option was to pray for wisdom on managing the chaos before it got out of hand. I won on certain issues, and lost some, but mostly I learnt great lessons.

Lesson

As we progress in life's journey, the Lord uses people to teach and correct us using situations. **Every season is beautiful on its own, either difficult, challenging, or smooth. Their distinct beauty makes the next season worthwhile.** Summer season allows us to enjoy the beauty of the sun and its warmth. Hot weather causes us to appreciate winter, where we can focus on ourselves, embrace the comfort of home, and enjoy various relationships. It's a season of recovery and preparation, they say, assessing the various

40 Lessons in 40 in Years | 197

occurrences throughout the year to determine vision for the next.

This new season may have been challenging for me being in an unknown place, with unfamiliar family members who might be going through the same. I appreciated the exposure and experience of a big family, learning to disagree to agree—the wisdom in handling sensitive conversations and, mostly, the need to keep quiet.

Ecclesiastes 3:11-13 EASY

God gave us the ability to think about his world, but we can never completely understand everything he does. And yet, he does everything at just the right time.

I learned that the best thing for people to do is to be happy and enjoy themselves as long as they live. God wants everyone to eat, drink, and enjoy their work. These are gifts from God.

When it comes to seasons, we often dwell too much on the past or rush into the future when we should be seizing the present and embracing all the wisdom it offers. This way, when the future arrives at our next destination, we are well prepared for what lies ahead.

It was a time of getting to know myself and my in-laws, but mostly, it was a season of learning to adopt and accept the family I had married into.

Ruth 1:19-20NIV

So, the two women went on until they came to Bethlehem. When they arrived in Bethlehem, the whole town was stirred because of them, and the women exclaimed, "Can this be Naomi?"

"Don't call me Naomi," she told them. "Call me Mara, because the Almighty[ᶜ] has made my life very bitter. I went away full, but the LORD has brought me back empty. Why call me Naomi? The LORD has afflicted[ᵉ] me; the Almighty has brought misfortune upon me."

Ruth 4:14-15NIV

The women said to Naomi: "Praise be to the LORD, who this day has not left you without a guardian-redeemer. May he become famous throughout Israel! He will renew your life and sustain you in your old age. For your daughter-in-law, who loves you and who is better to you than seven sons, has given him birth."

Naomi and Ruth embarked on a journey they never expected anything positive considering the calamity of losing their husbands. However, amid uncertainty, they journeyed not knowing what was in store for them. To them, it was an end to a painful season; in God, it was the beginning of a generational blessing.

Lesson 34: Becoming a Mummy

A week before my due date, contractions began at midnight. It was agonising in the night and then by morning the pain would subside as if nothing had happened. There were some days we would drive to the hospital in the hope that the baby was coming out, but on getting there, the contractions would cease and there would be no dilation at all after being checked.

This continued for the whole week. We were going back and forth to the hospital. I lost energy as I couldn't eat anything except liquid foods. Everyone was getting fed up and stressed. It looked like I was pretending the whole process as I will be in severe pain at night and the pain will totally die off by morning.

On this faithful day, I was exhausted with the back and forth. I thought I was losing my life or that of my child. When we got to the hospital, I had to transfer my frustration to the nurses, telling them I was not leaving the hospital without them finding a solution. If anything happened to me or my child, I would hold them responsible.

I then realised they didn't have much of my hospital records, so they didn't want to be responsible for any incident. They were just waiting for the baby to pop out.

Gracefully, the baby arrived the next morning. It was such a relief to see the baby finally out. However, she wouldn't cry whatsoever. I could see the nurse's running helter-skelter, but I was dazed with an epidural injection in my system. I had requested it due to inadequate strength to push the baby out.

It was taking too long to hear anything or the cry of a baby. Not hearing a thing from them was becoming frustrating. I then prompted my mother-in-law who was sitting across the room to check on the nurses if everything was alright.

As my mother-in-law got closer to enquire, they confirmed all was okay. They just needed to make sure the baby's health was intact. Before that, they had taken out liquid from the head, examining the baby's health, and the result was negative. I did not know what this meant but thank God the baby was alright.

In hindsight, the baby came out a girl rather than the boy we were expecting. I was excited that my discernment had materialised. It felt like I was carrying a girl than a boy. A few months before my giving birth, we received a prophetic word that there was a boy around my husband, so everyone concluded I was carrying a boy but I felt different. Little did we know that that was for the future. My mother-in-law couldn't contain her joy. She wanted a girl as well.

Right at the hospital, we changed her name as we had a boy's name planned. Her arrival changed everything and that was the beginning of an unfolding story. To God be all the glory for everything he has done.

Lesson

The baby's arrival affirmed that God will always make things happen at his own predestined time. My contractions started a week earlier, so we thought the baby would arrive earlier than expected. Rather, it was for our preparation. **Some things look like the main course, whereas it's an appetiser towards the main meal. Some breakthroughs come hidden behind a deceptive conclusion.**

Following on to the prophecy, we couldn't determine the sex of the baby when we went for our scan, as the baby would not open for the scan to capture in between its legs, so all they held on to was the prophetic word, except me. Prior to baby's arrival, I would sit at a clothing shop for hours admiring girls' clothing than I would for boys' clothing. I ended up buying whites and creams baby clothing.

The Lord will always speak to us in a manner we will never miss if only we can trust the still, silent voice whispering in our hearts. He loves us too much to leave us wondering and searching for answers without giving us a clue.

Deuteronomy 31:8 EASY

The Lord himself goes in front of you. He will always be with you, to help you. He will never leave you. So do not be afraid. Be brave!'

Numbers 23:19EASY

God is not human. He does not tell lies. He does not change his thoughts. If he promises to do something, it happens.

Lesson: 35 Broken

We were blessed with our second child. We had a boy whose arrival fulfilled the prophetic word spoken before his arrival. The Lord was gracious to us through thick and thin before. I can't fathom how we went through it all, but all I can say is God has been faithful.

Amid gratitude, the reality was inevitable. I was uncertain about the future as distance continued to affect the marriage. We existed instead of living. Our kids became the centre of everything, and we were parenting from different sides. There were few to no conversations, no arguments but silence. Home was a lonely place, yet we were a family.

On several occasions, I would break the silence by asking if everything was alright, to see if something could be done differently. There would be little to no response most times. We kept going back and forth on this without any conclusion.

I sought the Lord to show and teach me how to handle this situation. It's easy to point fingers, count faults and play the blame game, however this does not resolve any situation. The best place to turn for better resolution is to speak to God as my strength was exhausted. I prayed for wisdom.

I wanted to understand what was pulling my husband's attention so I prayed to God to show me how to rectify it even, if it was my fault.

I discerned that something was wrong but couldn't place a finger on it. Blaming it on an intruder was easy yet indescribable. There was constant dryness in our family life. Nothing was increasing, there were barriers to progress, and it was from one struggle to another. I did not see the providence of God in our home.

My spirit was continuously heavy; hope was dying away, and my only prayer was that the Lord would show me the way out of my helplessness. I needed answers to this prevalence, and I wanted to understand the correct posture in response to this, as I could foresee that my marriage was collapsing.

One evening, I felt strongly about going on the internet using our laptop. As I browsed, I stumbled on downloaded videos, and to my surprise, these were porn videos. The sight of downloaded porn was estranging, but to see different kinds and method of porn was a total knockout. Further to that, there was one which had been recently watched halfway before I saw it. Some of them had been deleted and were in the recycle bin, which meant it was an ongoing occurrence. I decided to search through the laptop for enough evidence, as I couldn't believe what I was seeing. I read chats on Skype messenger where my husband had had with other partners talking about their experiences. My adrenaline was turned upside down.

Faced with reality, what do I do, what did I do wrong, where some of the questions that run through my mind. When I vowed "for better for worse", I never imagined it could be this kind of worse.

Lesson

In between discovery and manifestation is preparation. How prepared are you for what is yet to happen? How prepared are you willing to allow yourself to go through the journey of the unknown without breaking down? **The question is not about whether we are broken or not. The issue is about how we respond to what broke us.** Do we leave it alone in that state? Do we try to mend what has been broken? Or do we walk away pretending nothing occurred? How far and how soon are we willing for what's broken to mend? How soon are we willing to accept that what happened really happened? Playing the blame game will not resolve anything, but navigating the way forward to recovery is important.

Amid my confusion, I remembered I was in prayer; therefore, the evidence of my prayer is this discovery. The only thing that helped me was the assurance that God is with me. His faithfulness is irrefutable, and I had assurance that it would soon be over.

Someone would ask, did you pray about your marriage? How sure were you that you were supposed to marry this person?

At this point, my confidence was in the fact that I prayed as much as I could, and if God allowed this to happen, He had a plan for me. **The fact that you are praying about something does not mean it will happen in the same manner as your prayer. To pray about something means**

210

allowing God's will to manifest. It is not just about you. It is about His will for our life's manifestation, becoming what He purposed.

He created Adam and Eve, placed them in the Garden of Eden, and gave them specific instructions, knowing that they would certainly disobey, yet he allowed them to make a choice.

There is always an Eden for every believer. He gives us instructions and His word, but we are allowed to make choices for ourselves. We have the free will. As much as he is aware of our choice, His arms are open just in case we choose Him. He is not aiming for our destruction but to allow our intentionality. He wants to relate with us at our level.

Even though my innocence was painfully played on, the love of God catered for that progressively. He intervened miraculously like nothing had ever happened.

Genesis 2: 15-17 NKJV

Then the LORD *God took the man and put him in the garden of Eden to tend and keep it. And the* LORD *God commanded the man, saying, "Of every tree of the garden you may freely eat; but of the tree of the knowledge of good and evil you shall not eat, for in the day that you eat of it you shall surely die."*

John 5:6 NKJV

When Jesus saw him lying there, and knew that he already had been in that condition a long time, He said to him, "Do you want to be made well?"

We will be asked and answer this question as we journey with God, and our sincere answer determines our trust in Him even when it hurts. How would you respond?

Lesson 36: Tip of the Iceberg

For days, I could not believe what I just discovered. I discerned something was wrong, yet I couldn't place my finger on what was happening. I had convictions, even my concerned friends had also told me likewise, but I insisted on waiting for vivid information to back it up. I prayed for more evidence than chats and video downloads on a laptop device as this could be a frame-up.

One faithful night, I left home for work as usual. On my way, I was engaged in a call with a friend, which took over most of the journey. As I was approaching my work venue, a call came from one of my supervisors saying that my shift had been cancelled as the client was not available, which meant I had to return home.

On my way home, I called the friend back, and we continued our conversation. It was quite a long discussion that I forgot to notify my husband that my shift had been cancelled that day.

I was happy to be at home with family, sleeping on my bed throughout the night, as I worked night shift at the time.

I opened our door with my key, and behold, what I feared had come upon me, and just like Job in the Bible had exclaimed that what he feared had manifested right in front of him. I was here, standing before my fears as much as I wanted to see it.

Someone was in our bedroom with my husband, I believe upon my arrival and probably hearing me questioning my husband why he dashed out half naked from our bedroom, the person went to hide in our bathroom, our bedroom is an ensuite. As I entered in curiosity to understand why my husband came out half naked, I saw evidence of intimate acts everywhere in the bedroom that I could not fathom how this was possible. Amid me screaming for answers from my husband, the person run out from the bathroom, grabbed his stuff as quick as he can including my handbag that was laying on the floor and run out of the house.

Our neighbours heard the noise and called the police. The police came into our house and took my husband away for that night. I remained in shock throughout the night and, for days, still couldn't believe that sight. After his return, there was total silence. I was broken, lost for options and couldn't control my tears. I had never felt this humiliated in my life.

That is exactly what I needed to see. It was no longer a case of perhaps. It was a matter of reality. Right at that point, I needed to decide on how I wanted to respond to this finding. As I already felt useless and worthless as a woman. I realised I had been a cover-up wife throughout the marriage.

Lesson

Anytime you start praying about anything, you invite heaven into the matter. The moment you position yourself to want to receive, with the correct posture of mind and emotion, you are bound to receive. **The Lord might reveal secrets that may demand a different aspect of yourself to assimilate and embrace.**

You will need to be emotionally and psychologically ready for what is being revealed to you, so you don't break down due to the weight of what you discover, to preserve what has been shared. God will certainly prepare you for any breakthrough, by dropping them in digestible nuggets. They may come as knowing, dreams, or words of knowledge. **The Lord will not reveal fully until He knows we can process and**

accommodate what's been released. Therefore, when we are praying for answers and we are yet to receive them, it might be because we are not ready for the weight of what will be revealed, knowing that his word does not go out without accomplishment. When the Lord speaks or sends forth His word, it does not go out void.

Isaiah 55:10-11BSB

For just as rain and snow fall from heaven and do not return without watering the earth, making it bud and sprout, and providing seed to sow and food to eat, so My word that proceeds from My mouth will not return to Me empty, but it will accomplish what I please, and it will prosper where I send it.

After seeing what I saw, unable to comprehend the brokenness, I began professing negatively of myself. I thought I married the man who truly loved me, who saw me as the best thing that could ever happen to Him. Well, he said all those and more, but what I saw didn't look like his promise. To compete with another person over what is legally and spiritually yours is unbearably painful. I couldn't comprehend it all. Like Hagar in the scriptures, after being used to produce a baby, she was now wallowing in the desert, stuck in the middle.

Genesis 21:17-19 ESV

And God heard the voice of the boy, and the angel of God called to Hagar from heaven and said to her, "What troubles you, Hagar? Fear not, for God has heard the voice of the boy where he is. Up! Lift up the boy, and hold him fast with your hand, for I will make him into a great nation." Then God opened her eyes, and she saw a well of water. And she went and filled the skin with water and gave the boy a drink.

Baby Ishmael, cried out to God though not the child with the promise, yet the Lord out of His mercy heard him by providing Hager with the secret code to her dilemma in the wilderness. The wilderness is not a place of destruction. It is a place where secrets are revealed if well managed, where men come into acquaintance with whom God has already called them to be.

As much as I didn't directly receive what I was supposed to do at this point, in prayer and worship, I felt the peace of God. I believed God had my back. I believed He was working out something that was yet to be revealed. Knowing He loved me, and that I was in His plan was enough to keep me going. I had confidence in knowing that God would do what He had purposed to do right from the start of the marriage, and I was ready to see it.

Lesson 37: Breaking Point

We moved out of London towards the West Midlands of London as the living expenses were affordable there. I got a new job. I decided not to allow these conditions to hold me back. I decided to walk through it, trusting God for direction as I journeyed. What I saw was not forgotten, it changed my demeanour in the marriage. He never explained why he did what he did; he faked apologies but never stopped. We grew further apart as I understood I was just a cover-up bride.

One day after we had moved, I woke up in the middle of the night to go to the toilet. While sitting on the toilet to ease myself, I saw something I hadn't seen before in the bathroom. Surprised at the sight of it, I decided to open the container to verify its content. I saw something like broken crystal content in a medicine container, hidden behind the toilet bowl. I didn't want to conclude anything, so I gathered the courage, took a portion of it in a tissue, took it to work, and showed it to a few guys I thought might know what it was. After asking around, someone confirmed it could be Crystal methamphetamines (Crystal Meth). That can't be true, I exclaimed. I must be dreaming, no it can't be, I told myself in denial.

Before this discovery, the person I knew well had become a total stranger. I couldn't understand anything he did or said. He was always accusing me of hacking into his phone and laptop. He shouted at me for no reason, demanding money for things I didn't see the need for. I was in a dilemma.

Things started getting worse. He burned the children's toys, saying there was something in it monitoring him. I remember him screaming very early in the morning, saying his spirit was leaving his body. There were several incidents in different episodes that were humiliating and didn't make sense at the time. I asked him several times to explain what was happening, but he couldn't give any reasonable explanation.

As I understood what was wrong with him, I booked a rehabilitation centre for him to see if he could be helped or get some support, but to no avail.

His threats were getting out of hand. I couldn't sleep, neither could the kids. The humiliation was unbearable as he constantly had harmful things like hammer, scissors etc saying someone was hacking his phone. It was very difficult to go to work as I was constantly in fear of losing my life or possibly hurting any of our children. He wouldn't sleep or eat. I panicked, leaving the kids with him, or allowing him to pick them up from school. I had to figure out school runs, and with working full time and paying the bills, I was depressed.

One day, I got home, not knowing what episode was waiting for me. I surprisingly got home and met their absence. Food for the kids was still in the kitchen. I called his phone. It started ringing in the living room. Ooh dear! he left his phone at home. I began panicking, not knowing where they were. I didn't know what his intentions were or if they were safe. This is me at 6 pm, calling everyone we knew and asking if they had visited, but to no avail. I called Pastor Mario, our family friend who came with me in search of them everywhere I knew they could be but to no avail.

As at 8 pm, I had lost it, I had no option but to call the police. I called the police, and they intervened in the search. The Police assured me that they would be found. Around 9 p.m., Pastor Mario who was still with me got a call from the police asking if he knew who my husband was. He confirmed and added that we were looking for them. Shortly after that, we met them at a given location. When we got there, we saw ambulances doing checks on him to see if he was okay, as the neighbours of that area had reported unreasonable behaviour. My details were confirmed as the children's mother, and they safely handed them to me. This incident was referred to the social services.

Lesson

My days were full of planning the next move and how this situation would be resolved. I feared what the future hold and had lost hope. I asked myself, where did I go wrong? What could I have done better? I needed answers but couldn't place my hand on anything reasonable except to keep trusting God for a miracle, notwithstanding the uncertainty.

Amid all this, my survival mode was activated. I just needed to survive and have my sanity intact as I sense I was losing it. I understood that someone had made a choice, and I had to make mine too, not just for myself but for the innocent children dependent on me. They are relying on my sanity for their upbringing.

When God is leading your journey, be ready for disruption. There are times he calms the storm by simply commanding the storm to cease, and there are times He allows us to be thrown out of the boat for peace in the boat. **The fact that you've been thrown out of the boat does not mean you are at a loss. Rather, you have come to the end of that journey. It's a sign of a closed chapter.** Wait for the new chapter to open. It is already budding, hang in there for your season of manifestation is here.

As much as Jonah was thrown out of the boat because of His disobedience, he also needed to be out because he was in the wrong direction. His assignment was at stake. God's will need fulfilment. His route needed to change in conformity to his call and purpose.

Jonah 1:14-15 NIV

Then they cried out to the LORD, "Please, LORD, do not let us die for taking this man's life. Do not hold us accountable for killing an innocent man, for you, LORD, have done as you pleased." Then they took Jonah and threw him overboard, and the raging sea grew calm.

Unfortunately, we don't get to decide our preferred option, He decides His will and how it will manifest.

As I was going through this turbulence, I couldn't pray much, and my fears had engulfed me. I didn't know what to pray but mostly spoke in tongues because at that point, I had exhausted all I knew to do to no avail. Worship songs were my go-to. I prepared and led praise and worship at church I was attending as if nothing was happening, but I was there for the mercies of God to prevail.

I knew the best decision was to get out of this storm, or else I would lose my mind, my life or one of our children. I felt all alone in the middle of the sea. I could not confide in anyone, as I knew the weight of my story was not for everyone, except the one sent as a helper. None of my family members knew what had been happening. I was too ashamed to voice it out. I carried my burden everywhere alone.

Remember, not everyone is assigned to you as a helper, don't be mad at them if you expected more from them. Understand they can only give what they have, and their willingness to offer any help will be through the prompting of the Holy Spirit. **If the Lord does not touch the heart of your helpers, they will not be bothered.**

John 3:27NIV

To this John replied, "A person can receive only what is given them from heaven.

Deuteronomy 31:6 NIV

*Be strong and courageous. Do not be afraid or terrified because of them, for the L*ORD *your God goes with you; he will never leave you nor forsake you."*

The Lord had promised that in any situation we find ourselves, He will not leave or forsake us. He is aware of the enemy's deeds and intentions towards mankind. As the Lord lives, trust Him, you will not be put to shame.

In times like this, the Lord will not bring many people. He will only bring those you truly need. Your most trusted folks may start pulling away. **Those we need will remain on post.** Do not be discouraged by it, as God will only allow what is, following His plans. Remember, He does not share his glory with anyone.

Isaiah 42:8-9 NLT

"I am the LORD; that is my name I will not give my glory to anyone else, nor share my praise with carved idols. Everything I prophesied has come true, and now I will prophesy again. I will tell you the future before it happens."

Acts 9:10-12 NIV.

In Damascus, there was a disciple named Ananias. The Lord called to him in a vision, "Ananias!" "Yes, Lord," he answered. The Lord told him, "Go to the house of Judas on Straight Street and ask for a man from Tarsus named Saul, for he is praying. In a vision, he has seen a man named Ananias come and place his hands on him to restore his sight."

If you remain in prayer, God will send a bail out, be encouraged.

Lesson 38: The Exit

The involvement of social workers was a breakthrough, bringing people who understand the implication of this case, who will advise the correct measures to remedy the situation without prejudice.

We had countless meetings, filling of forms and discussed strategy to keep myself and the kids safe. Each day came with a new adventure, therefore, I needed to be alert and be as close to an exit as possible or call the police in case anything triggered. This is because he walked around the house with a knife, hammer and lighter as a protection, because he thinks someone was after him.

One day, my case worker turned in for her usual appointment, It wasn't a good scene as an episode was going on. As she approached our house, my husband had already burnt a pile of toys with fire in our bedroom, saying something was in it that is monitoring him. The fire spread on the carpet on the floor, which nearly caused a fire emergency. Before this happened, my case worker had insisted I move out of my home as that environment was no longer safe for myself and the children. My home had become a death-trap.

As the toys burned in the bedroom, I quickly opened the door, ready for exit in case it got worse. Our son was crying for his burnt toys. My husband heard him crying, so he began shouting, asking me why our son was crying. He ran down the stairs as he spoke, with his eyes wild opened. He became very aggressive, wanting to take our son off me as I carried him and pulled away. The social worker walked in and upon seeing that scene, she had to intervene sternly, especially when she saw that he still had his knife and hammer with him.

The social worker was firm with her decisions, insisting I move out as we couldn't risk what can happen next. That was the third physical aggression involving the kids which could have resulted in harm. She said 'Charity, you must move out of here! It might be too late for you to escape if something happens.'

I reiterated that I didn't have anywhere to go and didn't know how I could cater for my two children, without working, having no recourse to government funds. They also needed to be in school. How was I going to handle all that without a helping hand? She explained I need safety first, she could arrange a refuge centre for us, so I should think it through and feed her back when I was ready.

A few days later, my husband woke me up in the middle of the night asking me for money and his phone. He said he couldn't find his phone and needed money to pay for an over six-hundred-pound car insurance debt. Firstly, why should this be brought up in the middle of the night? Secondly, the car was taken by the police that night he went missing with the kids as the insurance on the car had been cancelled. As I was explaining this to him, he started shouting, threatening to slap, and hit me with the hammer if I didn't give him money. He relented for a while as I had no money to give him. I was scared for my life and thought I was going to die at that moment. I called my friend, Mrs Ernestina Tsiquaye, who had just moved to the US from the UK. Briefly, I told her what had been happening. We held on to the phone and prayed till morning.

I brought the kids downstairs and made them sleep on the couch. I sat as close to the door as possible and was attentive to his movements upstairs just in case, he did anything fishy. I was waiting for morning to speak with the social worker.

I agreed to go to the refuge as I didn't see myself alive in that house for another day. While on the phone with Mrs Tsiquaye, she spoke to her other friend, who allowed us into her house while the social worker arranged for a refuge centre. The kids and I stayed with the friend for three days. By the first week of July 2019, we journeyed to the refuge centre.

Lesson

In the thick of this turbulence, one thing stuck with me. **I know God will not lead us to where there is no provision, even if it's in the lion's den.** When the social worker began talking to me about refuge, I didn't just jump into it because I knew that the moment I stepped out of the door, that would be the end of the marriage so it was important for me to divinely confirm God's will. My prayer was for God to give me a sign for this exit or intervene.

As I prayed, I was also afraid for him as well. What would be his fate? Was he not going to hurt himself? Is he going to get better? But in everything, there was this peace within me that God would take care of him also. I have never stopped praying for our healing and I trust that God will reach us wherever we are.

God has you in the palm of his hand. He promises that though we walk through the valley of the shadow of death we should fear no evil, for He is with us. His staff and His rod guard and lead us through.

Psalm 23:4NIV

Even though I walk through the darkest valley, I will fear no evil, for you are with me; your rod and your staff, they comfort me.

When it was Israel's season to exit Egypt, something had to happen for the exit to take place. Pharaoh's heart was hardened for the power of God to prevail. He needed to know

God's power and might. **For us to exit an unbearable circumstance, there must be disruption.**

Sometimes, God answers prayers by allowing turbulences to occur. He heard the prayer of Israel after 420 years of slavery. He called a person, prophet Moses, to lead Israel from slavery. He created a whole human being just for this purpose. Even though it took a while for God's response, it was still in accordance with His will and season. He remembered His covenant with Abraham, Isaac, and Jacob. He could no longer watch Pharaoh's dominance over his people. **When the voice of covenant cries out for help, the Lord intervenes by sending a Man.**

Exodus 3:6-10 NLT

I am the God of your father—the God of Abraham, the God of Isaac, and the God of Jacob."
When Moses heard this, he covered his face

because he was afraid to look at God. Then the LORD told him, "I have certainly seen the oppression of my people in Egypt. I have heard their cries of distress because of their harsh slave drivers. Yes, I am aware of their suffering. So, I have come down to rescue them from the power of the Egyptians and lead them out of Egypt into their own fertile and spacious land. It is a land flowing with milk and honey—the land where the Canaanites, Hittites, Amorites, Perizzites, Hivites, and Jebusites now live. Look! The cry of the people of Israel has reached me, and I have seen how harshly the Egyptians abuse them. Now go, for I am sending you to Pharaoh. You must lead my people Israel out of Egypt."

Just as the Lord intervened for Israel, His beloved nation, he intervened on my behalf. He will see you through thick and thin. Remain steadfast on His promises and keep on in prayers. **When the time of the Lord is due, He will show up, be encouraged.**

You may want to quit because of Gods silence, but there will never be a time God is unreachable. The thought that God has rejected us is the enemy's weapon to keep us bound. **We can't let go of hope, for when hope is gone, we lose everything.**

Lesson 39: Life in the Refuge

We were given a train ticket to a town I had never heard of. I later realised it was about an hour-long journey on the train from Coventry. We were not told the location or postcode of our destination for safety reasons but asked to call and wait at the train station for someone to come and pick us up. A beautiful lady came to pick us up to our venue in no time.

We stopped at a Charity café to have lunch. After that, she took us to another part of the café, which is a food bank. As my bag was filled with food, I couldn't hold back my tears, thinking of how my life had turned around. It was heartbreaking to think that I would be depending on a food bank to feed my children. The truth was, I didn't have enough money on me, as I had not been paid for that month. I only took a suitcase containing few change clothes and toiletries with me, but the peace in my heart and the thought that God was in charge was my source of strength. The thought that I have life and didn't lose any of my children encouraged me to persevere in prayer of thanksgiving, taking each day at a time as the challenges rolled over.

We got to the refuge centre, went through registration, and a room was allocated to us. As empty as the room was, I still found rest knowing that God would sustain me through it all.

We started making friends. We familiarised ourselves with the town since the kids won't be in school till it opens in September. There, the journey to healing and recovery began.

Prayer and worship never ceased from my mouth; my only source of deliverance was in God. I prayed for mercy and healing for the entire household.

Lesson

My prayer was intense at the refuge, my spiritual hearing was clearer without ambiguity and doubt. The sound of his words brought me to my knees.

Before I went to the refuge centre, I was full of fear and anxiety. The future felt bleak, and the question of how I would survive this single life with children came to my mind. How do I take care of them and how will my life turn out? Thanks be to God for all mercies. He spoke his goodness into my spirit, and affirmed my calling into ministry, purpose, and the correct definition of this season. He gave me further information about The Covenant Esthers, a ministry he spoke to me about in 2017, but I didn't have the courage or peace of mind to carry it out. I also received the instruction to write this book. **In the place of seclusion God speaks.**

In our pain lies purpose. Acknowledge the birthing of purpose, as you tear in pain.

Don't just walk away in pain, leaving "purpose" behind, but allow "purpose" to journey with you. Investigate the lessons from each pain. Life is like a bicycle. As we sit to ride on it, both wheels are in motion. Each wheel represents different seasons of our life, both bad and good. So, as we journey through, they both come along, even in the worst days, we can identify some good. Investigate each occurrence to identify how they affect us so we can extract lessons from them. In times like these, we hold on to hope in God, knowing that He will not let us go unsecured, without assuring us of His good thoughts towards us.

Just like natural storms, personal storms can arrive quite unexpectedly. They don't make appointments. Like Job, every one of us has experienced situations we have no control over, situations we did not expect and could not prevent. Storms should not define our lives, rather they should be the stepping stone to rejuvenate.

Talk to God about your fears and every challenge because the greatest experience in life can be the best opportunity for renewal and liberation if we pray.

James 1:2-8 NKJV

My brethren, count it all joy when you fall into various trials, knowing that the testing of your faith produces patience. But let patience have its perfect work, that you may be perfect and complete, lacking nothing. If any of you lacks wisdom, let him ask of God, who gives to all liberally and without reproach, and it will be given to him. But let him ask in faith, with no doubting, for he who doubts is like a wave of the sea driven and tossed by the wind. For let not that man suppose that he will receive anything from the Lord; he is a double-minded man, unstable in all his ways.

Job 22:21 NLT

"Submit to God, and you will have peace; then things will go well for you.

Lesson 40: Rebuilding the Broken Pieces

The refuge became our new home with lovely women who had gone through similar trials and were walking the path to finding themselves. Despite this, some had already given up on hope and had a blurred vision of the future. Some had been inflicted so much that its impact had diminished their mental faculties. They were existing and had stopped living.

Those experiences encouraged me not to give up on hope. I allowed myself to be broken yet hoped for healing. I accepted this as part of my journey but not my destination. Accepting our brokenness means we are giving God something to work with. The area that gets broken creates a crack, which becomes the entrance for God's light to penetrate.

I had various therapeutic sessions, discussing what transpired, and considering different perspectives with its implications. I however deduced that God's intervention averted its consequences, which is my reason for gratitude, understanding that it could have been worse. It changed the trajectory of everything for me. I was encouraged by the other women's experiences and how they walked their journey to healing.

As we approached the end of the year 2019, the pandemic COVID-19 emerged, and the world was on lockdown which elongated our stay at the refuge. It took longer for government agencies to process our documents for relocation. However, God was faithful irrespective of the hiccups and delays.

The Covenant Esther's took off at the refuge when the introduction of live streaming apps allowed smooth conveyance of the gospel as people can join meetings virtually. I started virtual Bible Study and various programmes as instructed by the Holy Spirit weekly. We also attended Elim Church who were a great support to us at the refuge.

It is a joy and privilege to be seen by God and be assigned a role in His Kingdom. I wouldn't exchange that for anything. God saw me in the wilderness. He didn't just provide for me; He gave me directions to each season. Glory to God.

After 15 months in the refuge, we were allocated a house. The season of rebuilding the broken pieces began. I gained confidence and became conscious of my environment, opting for healing measures rather than dwelling on the past.

Lesson

The deepest things I have learned from my life are from my deepest suffering- Elizabeth Elliot.

Sometimes God allows people to leave and disappoint us not only for rejection's sake, but to allow us to grow. It creates space for a new season to shine forth, especially when such experience has the potential of sabotaging God's will for us. God may allow this to happen knowing it will do us good.

Genesis 50:20 BSB

As for you, what you intended against me for evil, God intended for good, in order to accomplish a day like this—to preserve the lives of many people.

There are times we expect some trusted people to journey with us in our pain but can't find them. We feel they should be with us in that safe space of friendship, but we are left by ourselves to figure healing out. It is very lonely. This is not the season to be bitter about their rejection but a season of growth, making room for God to be God. Allow Him to show us that His goodness, faithfulness, and his promise "I will not leave you nor forsake you" still works.

Deuteronomy 31:6 BSB

Be strong and courageous; do not be afraid or terrified of them, for it is the LORD your God who goes with you; He will never leave you nor forsake you.

The season of separation is the season of self, building the capacity to contend for what's been accorded to you through faith and consistency.

Understanding that as He made a way for your escape, He will guide and protect you through your wilderness journey to the unknown places. It is the Lord that goes with you, and you are His.

Deuteronomy 31:8 BSB

The LORD *himself goes before you and will be with you; he will never leave you nor forsake you. Do not be afraid; do not be discouraged."*

Don't let your mind wander on things he has not promised, the trash and lies from the enemy, speaking into your mind, causing fear and anxiety. Rather dwell on His promises, align your faith to His word, believing His word is true and will bring you to a perfect end.

Jeremiah 29:11 AMP

For I know the plans and thoughts that I have for you,' says the LORD, *'plans for peace and well-being and not for disaster, to give you a future and a hope.*

CONCLUSION

This book is my personal road map with God. It is also my testimony of how God has been good to me in diverse ways beyond comprehension. It is to attest Gods faithfulness in my journey in other to encourage anyone who feels God has deserted them and are considering giving up on hope, Gods deliverance and restoration. To encourage anyone experiencing life in a way that makes them question God's love and Fatherhood.

Amos 3:3 NLT

Can two people walk together without agreeing on the direction?

This clarifies that relationships can only work when both parties agree on a journey. Likewise, without God's will, we will be journeying life outside of His covering.

The same applies in the context of marriage. The Man is to unite with his wife and become one not as two. The idea of divorce should be out of discussion, however because of mans hardened heart, and our unwillingness to repent of our character, we have fallen into the enemy's agenda of divorce and separation. Unfaithfulness is the only reason we may consider divorce, nevertheless we can still repent, forgive, and rekindle the marriage provided the faulted partner is willing to.

Matt 19:3-9NKJV

The Pharisees also came to Him, testing Him, and saying to Him, "Is it lawful for a man to divorce his wife for just any reason?" And He answered and said to them, "Have you not read that He who made them at the beginning 'made them male and female,' and said, 'For this reason a man shall leave his father and mother and be joined to his wife, and the two shall become one flesh'? So then, they are no longer two but one flesh. Therefore, what God has joined together, let not man separate." They said to Him, "Why then did Moses command to give a certificate of divorce, and to put her away?"

He said to them, "Moses, because of the hardness of your hearts, permitted you to divorce your wives, but from the beginning it was not so. And I say to you, whoever divorces his wife, except for sexual immorality, and marries another, commits adultery; and whoever marries her who is divorced commits adultery."

How are we fulfilled or align our children when a partner decides to deviate from the covenant on which marriage is instituted?

God stated He hates divorce in Malachi 2:16, because it will be against His vision for marriage, becoming one flesh, living in harmony, without breaking the chord of marriage which is husband, wife, and God.

He also hates it when people choose to go after other gods, i.e allowing the love for other things to stray them from the love of God, without repenting. He said, He will bring to judgement and punish every unrepentant sin, Eccl. 12:14, Amos 1:13-15. Therefore, if marriage is not built on the word of God, it will not last.

We are accountable for the privileges in the divine economy of God. If we underestimate these privileges, we can't escape its consequences. The grace of God is an opportunity to repent, not a reason to remain unrepentant. When we build idols, i.e., things that are more important to us than loving him, we invite God's destruction.

In my case, we needed to go our separate ways because our path had taken another course, different from God's intent for marriage.

I prayerfully considered it, forgave, and resolved in my heart that it was time to let go, it was time to stop covering what needs exposing, allowing God's mediation and healing. I realised I was standing in the way, doing everything to maintain the marriage but the longer I remained in the broken environment, the more I got broken.

I am still benefiting from Gods promise of never leaving or forsaking me. He led me to another church where I fellowship and serve trusting God each day for my healing and wholeness.

As a child of God, wherever you find yourself, you must see fruitfulness, blessing, and multiplication. Depending on our destination, each experience in God propels our hearts towards purpose. The goodness and mercies of God will propel you into his plan. It will arrest your intuition so much that you will have no option but to run to him. Those who are after God's heart are in constant pursuit of his love.

His love is without repentance. He is constantly ensuring that He is within our reach so we can find him. There is a hope our hearts have been yearning for, the light to our dark path, and the answer to everything which is Jesus Christ. If we can find Him, we have won victoriously. He will remould you according to his perfection, until he finds you in his kingdom forever.

Here is my story of how God sustained me throughout my pain. How He redeemed me from shame, and rejection to how He is restoring everything the enemy had stolen.

Just as Joseph said in Gen 50:20, they meant it for evil, but God meant It for good. The plot of the enemy has turned around in my favour. Today, I sing of His goodness.

HALLELUYAH

Genesis 50:20 CEV

You tried to harm me, but God made it turn out for the best, so that he could save all these people, as he is now doing.

REFERENCE

Crushing by T.D Jakes-God turns Pressure into Power

The tide turning power of Hope-Good Catastrophe by Benjamin Windle

Adapted from Unexpected: Leave Fear Behind, Move Forward in Faith, Embrace the Adventure *by* Christine Caine. Copyright © 2018 by Christine Caine.

Mission Assist, P.O Box 257, Evesham, Worcestershire, England. WR11 9AW

Berean Study Bible @Bible Hub, 2022

ABOUT THE AUTHOR

Charity Mamealuwa Jumbo is originally from the western region of Ghana-West Africa through her paternal lineage, with roots in Nigeria. She also has ties to the Ashanti region of Ghana through her maternal family. She resides in the United Kingdom with her family, skilfully balancing her career, ministry, and family life. She is a mother of two wonderful children.

Charity is a devout woman of faith, and her continuous spiritual journey has led her to fulfil God's purpose for her life. This journey has culminated in the authorship of her debut book, "40 Lessons in 40 Years: 40 Years of God's Goodness."

Additionally, Charity founded "The Covenant Esthers," a ministry that gathers individuals with a divine calling on their lives. Through prayer and Bible study, this ministry supports and empowers those seeking to fulfil their God-ordained destinies. It serves as a guiding influence, much like Mordecai to Esther, helping individuals build their faith through the Word of God.

Charity also serves as the praise and worship minister for Todah City Church in Coventry, United Kingdom, under the leadership of Pastor Mario Ajavon. She has been blessed with opportunities to minister on various platforms, both in songs and in word.

ABOUT THE BOOK

Within life experiences lie valuable lessons, and how we recount these incidents plays a pivotal role in the wisdom we ultimately extract from them. I firmly believe that the events in my life were not mere coincidences but rather a carefully charted path by God, gradually unveiling His purpose for my existence.

'40 Lessons in 40 Years' beautifully captures my spiritual journey and the invaluable insights I gleaned from my walk with God. It delves into how He sustained me through the most trying moments of my marriage and redeemed me from the grips of domestic violence through a refuge shelter in the UK. This journey also showcases God's remarkable transformative power by which He restored and transformed my shattered life into a vessel of purpose.

While it took me four decades to accumulate these lessons, their true value stems from the goodness of the Lord. It's truly astonishing how God's goodness can lead us to uncharted and, at times, disturbing destinations and yet emerge with a refined purpose. He created the blacksmith who ignites the coals and fashions the weapon for its purpose, and the destroyer who wreaks havoc. In all circumstances, whether pleasant or challenging, we find assurance in Christ that no weapon formed against us shall prosper. God's goodness upholds and steers us until we embody His divine plan. Without His goodness, we are like smoking flax.

As we embark on the journey of becoming, we cannot fully become without the goodness of God.

Printed in Great Britain
by Amazon

37341886R00149